SUGGESTIVE-ACCELERATIVE LEARNING AND TEACHING

The Instructional Design Library

Volume 36

SUGGESTIVE-ACCELERATIVE LEARNING AND TEACHING

Owen L. Caskey

College of Education

Texas Tech University

Lubbock, Texas

Danny G. Langdon

Series Editor

Educational Technology Publications

Englewood Cliffs, New Jersey 07632

ANGLE

Library of Congress Cataloging in Publication Data

Caskey, Owen L
    Suggestive-accelerative learning and teaching.

    (The Instructional design library; v. 36)
    Bibliography: p.
    1. Educational acceleration. 2. Mental suggestion.
I. Title. II. Series: Instructional design library;
v. 36.
LB3061.C37   370.15'2   79-26386
ISBN 0-87778-156-7

Printed in the United States of America.

Library of Congress Catalog Card Number: 79-26386.

International Standard Book Number: 0-87778-156-7.

First Printing: March, 1980.

FOREWORD

As one who has become acquainted with and developed many instructional designs, I am particularly impressed and intrigued with Suggestive-Accelerative Learning and Teaching. What you will find in this book is valuable in terms of the specific design itself, but, in addition, many of the ideas set forth by the author are sound principles and techniques to be employed in *any* instructional design. Reading this book at least twice is recommended. You are certain to acquire its basic components and structure the first time through, but the second reading allows time to reflect on the meaning and implications for other learning needs you are faced with solving.

The author has done a splendid job of writing. He probably best summarizes this design when he states that the Lozanov (the originator of Suggestive-Accelerative Learning) method "combines memory expansion and relaxation, creating an alert but relaxed state of mind, during which the anti-suggestive barriers are lowered and there is an increasing receptiveness of the individual to suggestion and retention of new information." This design purports to provide means for opening the mind to the reception of information by clearing away the mental barriers which often keep many of us from receiving information.

The reader of other volumes in The Instructional Design Library will note that this book is longer than most in the series. This is due primarily to the need to provide back-

v

ground detail on the origins of this instructional design and on the theory behind it. This design *is* very different from the generally accepted mode of operation in schools and training centers, even though many of its principles, as noted above, can be found in all good instructional designs. Thus, while various components may not be new, it is true that the overall conceptualization and the manner in which the components are assembled *are* new, and perhaps somewhat startling to many people. Given this departure from general practice, it was deemed necessary to provide more general and theoretical information than is standard in other books in this series.

In conclusion, and hopefully without predisposing your own thinking, my initial thoughts about this design were of being intrigued, impressed with its potential, and wondering if I could implement it myself. One of these days I am just going to have to try it.

Danny G. Langdon
Series Editor

PREFACE

This book is intended to present both the theoretical basis and the practical application of suggestive-accelerative learning. While no theory is conclusive and no research base can be regarded as final, suggestive-accelerative learning appears to be moving from its infancy into the growing pains of adolescence. By far the most researched academic application is in foreign language learning, which was the original application and the one which remains closest to the classic procedures. Due to the interests of investigators, research emphasis, practical application, and, again, the original development, more is known about the impact of suggestive-accelerative methods with adults and older students than with younger ones. Finally, the applications to realistic school settings and in typically taught academic areas are progressing both geographically and sequentially, in steadily increasing numbers.

Be that as it may, at this point there exists sufficient evidence to warrant not only a reasonable level of enthusiasm about the promise of suggestive-accelerative techniques, but also a dependable body of knowledge surrounding a number of methodological applications. There are, for example, numerous research reports in the available literature and even more conference and workshop proceedings which attest to the advantage of suggestive-accelerative methods in carefully controlled experimental studies. There are even more general reports of practical applications which appear to have been helpful and productive for both the students involved and acquisition of material. While one may not be as certain about the results of these less carefully controlled studies, they cannot be overlooked, since they serve to move the methodology toward greater application and a more definitively evaluated use. In truth, all practical applications must go beyond the limited research evidence available, or little beyond theoretical concern would ever result.

It is intended that the material and selected examples contained herein will provide sufficient knowledge about suggestive-accelerative methods to enable the teacher to evaluate its usefulness in the areas and with the students for whom he or she is concerned. Further, it is anticipated that the teacher will be adequately informed regarding the principles and process of suggestive-accelerative learning to develop or adapt the basic methodology to specific curriculum objectives and class goals. Finally, and hopefully, it will generate enough enthusiasm on the part of the reader to translate interest into motivation. The test of the latter, of course, will reside in how many teachers make the effort to use suggestive-accelerative approaches with the individuals and groups in their charge—not as a replacement for existing methods which are working effectively or as a substitute for fundamental learning techniques which have a high level of practicality and acceptance, but as yet another way to involve students in worthwhile and enjoyable learning activities. The objective of additional rather than replacement for suggestive-accelerative applications will more nearly reflect the practical possibilities and a reasonable level of expectation for the immediate future.

The need for general and specific guidelines for implementation is no more nor no less for suggestive-accelerative methods than for any other. The need to experience and experiment may be somewhat more critical. Many successful suggestive-accelerative learning and teaching (SALT) practitioners, however, began with far less than is currently available in the way of directions and applications. Our hope is that this brief overview will foster interest and activities among teachers at all educational levels.

The author gratefully acknowledges the assistance of numerous individuals who have helped with both the concepts and applications of suggestive-accelerative learning, particularly the classroom teachers who have been willing to employ the methodology with students in their charge. Special thanks go to Brenda Hayes for her general assistance and expert skills which made the preparation of this volume possible.

O. L. C.

CONTENTS

ABSTRACT

SUGGESTIVE-ACCELERATIVE LEARNING
AND TEACHING

Suggestive-accelerative learning and teaching is the American application of a unique methodology developed by Dr. Georgi Lozanov, a Bulgarian psychiatrist, who carried out extensive research in the 1960's, developing an approach to learning which combined memory expansion and relaxation designed to develop perceptive potential, increase concentration, and reduce stress and anxiety. In an elaborate series of experiments, primarily oriented around language learning, he found that students learned with less effort and retained more of the material which had been presented to them as a result of his highly effective instructional method. He termed the method of applying elements of suggestion theory to classroom learning as Suggestology, and the application of relaxation and suggestion techniques in learning settings as Suggestopedia.

Utilizing a unique combination of elements, including mental and physical relaxation, positive suggestions, music backgrounds, high multi-sensory input, and an emphasis on visual imagery, suggestive-accelerative approaches have been successful in increasing the amount of material learned in a given time or reducing the amount of time necessary to learn new material in a wide variety of subject matter areas at almost all educational levels. The organized use of such techniques theoretically permits information to be absorbed more readily by the individual by bypassing emotional barriers which accompany most learning activities, and it results in a larger percentage of learned material being retained in the long-term memory area of the brain. Learning is not only faster but more enjoyable, while resulting in high retention rates. In addition, the self-concept of the learner is enhanced both as a result of higher achievement and the positive suggestions which are a basic part of the suggestive-accelerative approach.

The adaptation of Suggestopedia, even in its Americanized version, to the typical classroom setting has required modification in both techniques and applications. The evidence to date, however, clearly indicates that increases in learning can occur through the use of the suggestive-accelerative elements in carefully planned classroom approaches. While it is obvious that suggestive-accelerative techniques work better with some subject matter areas than others and that many of its components are more easily applied in the classroom, the fact that such applications are compatible with the more current philosophies of education and developing methodological theories remains an important fact. Suggestive-accelerative learning is an effective procedural approach which does not prescribe what to teach, but provides a method which creates an optimum combination of conditions for effective learning to take place. The suggestive-accelerative techniques which have been found helpful in accelerating classroom learning involve interesting activities for both teacher and student. They are not meant to replace other techniques or approaches which have been traditionally a part of working with children in classrooms. The method includes elements which are familiar to all teachers yet involves approaches and activities which are relatively new. There is, at this time, a sizeable body of research and information concerning the results of suggestive-accelerative learning and an increasing level of enthusiasm which is both testimony to the practical applications which are reported and a promise for educational methodology to move even more toward student-centered classroom experiences.

SUGGESTIVE-ACCELERATIVE
LEARNING AND TEACHING

I.

USE

Introduction

Would you be interested in an approach which research indicates increases learning capacity and retention? One which does not require extensive training or a special setting? One which can be used with regular classes, small groups, or even in counseling? One which uses equipment available in most schools and requires little or no expenditure of funds? One which is easily explained, easily accepted, and generally supported by teachers and students? One which presents few, if any methodological, theoretical, or practical problems? One which includes several sound, time-tested elements, yet has aspects which keep it new and exciting? Idealistic? Of course! One would have to admit that a method meeting these criteria quite likely does not exist. One that may indeed approach the criteria, however, is called the suggestive-accelerative method.

Research indicates that, despite the apparently effortless learning setting in this instructional design, material coverage is five to 50 times more, with retention equal or exceeding traditional methods when suggestive-accelerative processes are employed. It seems that more material can be covered in the same time, or the same amount of material can be covered in much less time, depending on the needs of the learning group and setting. If you were an observer in a classroom using the suggestive-accelerative approach, your description might be that students are relaxed yet attentive, absorbing the material in an intuitive manner while listening to music. What is happening and why it works is a very complex matter which cannot adequately be covered in this brief publication. In a summary fashion, however, we would like to present an elementary review of suggestive-accelerative methods with some attention to the theoretical elements and procedural components. Primarily, the presentation of sample activities and guidelines for a variety of educational levels and academic areas will constitute a large part of the pages and sections that follow.

The suggestive-accelerative teaching method is an approach which utilizes a combination of elements in sequence to present material to students. A number of these elements have been used in isolation or in non-teaching settings over a number of years, but which when used in an organized and consistent way have been found to be effective in accelerating classroom learning. The technique involves a number of components, the more important of which are relaxation, visual imagery, positive suggestion, and a calming music background. Although there are earlier and common factors included in the process, in many ways suggestive-accelerative teaching is the Americanized version of Suggestology.

Suggestology (from the Latin *suggestio* and the Greek *logia*), defined as the scientific study of suggestion, with the term Suggestopedia meaning the application to teaching, was devised by the Bulgarian psychiatrist, Dr. Georgi Lozanov, and often is referred to as the Lozanov method. Lozanov, a recognized psychotherapist, became interested in suggestion in the 1950's and early 1960's as a member of the staff of the Post-Graduate Medical Institute in Bulgaria. His own description of his early work centered on the realization that there was no significant difference between the success rate of the various therapies being employed by the Department of Psychiatry, to which he was assigned. In an early attempt to relate patient preference to therapeutic technique, they would describe several basic approaches to incoming patients, primarily adults suffering from various neurotic conditions, and assign them to the therapy group which was felt to be most beneficial. They were, for example, given an opportunity to select from hypnotherapy, drug therapy, psychoanalysis, a Moreno type of psychodrama, and autogenic training. After over 350 chronic psychosomatic patients evidenced 76 percent remission of symptoms, Lozanov concluded that the patient's choice of therapy bore direct relationship to success in the therapeutic process. The patient's expectations of positive results were likely to be verified in a sort of self-suggestive process. Lozanov then expanded his interest in suggestion to the surgical field, developing what was called "thought anesthesia" and, in 1965, the Institute accepted this suggestion-based technique as an approved method for surgery in their medical clinics. In the late 1960's, he carried out a succession of experiments in relaxation, hypermnesia, hypnosis, and suggestion, using language learning and memorization in the research, which was typically a pre-post test, control-experimental group design.

In 1966, the Bulgarian Ministry of Education established the Scientific Research Institute of Suggestology in Sofia, Bulgaria, as a part of the University of Sofia, for the continuation of Lozanov's research. The experimental design and the direct application of the suggestopedic method was the teaching of foreign languages to adults. Using the Suggestopedic approach, almost 2,000 students completed language courses at the Research Institute of Suggestology between 1966 and 1971. While there were some variations in length and duration of the courses, the basic language classes were conducted for three to four hours per day, six days a week, for one month each. Three course sequences of this type were designed for teaching French, English, German, Italian, Spanish, and Russian. The first course typically covered up to 2,000 words, with a level of achievement equivalent to those occurring in traditional classes with over 300 hours of instruction. The three courses covering over 6,000 words in a three-month period are judged to approximate the grammar and vocabulary normally covered in a two- to three-year language course as taught in a more conventional fashion. Classes typically learned 80 to 100 new words per class session, although in some experimental situations over 500 new words were learned and retained with over 90 percent accuracy when tested three days later. In isolated experiments, it was reported that some students managed to cover 1,000 or more new words in a session, although the information concerning the details of such experiments is quite sparse.

Apart from the special research results, the important thing is that over the years, class after class has learned languages at rates ranging from five to 50 times those found in school and commercial classes. Surprisingly, there is little variation between students and across languages. Even more important is that retention rates were uniformly found to be approximately 95 percent when tested after one day and over 90 percent three days later, with no significant differences between the languages taught. This is in contrast to the general assumption regarding rates of retention (or forgetting) which have been accepted since the turn of the century, usually around 50 percent loss in one day and 75 percent loss after two days. Admittedly, such curves of forgetting have been based on abstract, often meaningless material (i.e., nonsense syllables, foreign words without definition, unrelated nouns or adjectives), but the difference in rates is still of considerable importance. The results obtained in the Institute classes prompted Lozanov to postulate on a "curve of recollection" as best describing the results of the Suggestopedic method, in which the long-term memory increases rather than diminishes. While this is not substantiated in whole, evidence indicates that the retention in language courses has been 88 percent after six months and a gradual linear reduction to 57 percent after almost two years. This becomes more impressive when one considers that there was little or no active use of the language during the intervening time. While there are many factors involved in such reports (the use of combined components of the method will be covered later, for example), the results are of sufficient importance to warrant attention to the method and its potential application to all types and levels of learning.

Lozanov's school applications began in 1970 when an experiment with 16-year-old boys in two Sofia schools found them completing the year's assigned academic work almost three months early while studying six hours a day without homework. By 1973, he had arranged for two large schools in Sofia and two comparison schools in rural Bulgaria to use his method to teach reading and mathematics in kindergarten, first, and second grades. At the end of the year, those taught with his method had significantly higher achievement. Understandably encouraged, 16 schools involving almost 3,000 students throughout Bulgaria were taught all academic subjects and the arts using his method in the 1975-1976 school year. In 1977-1978, it is estimated that 5,000 children at all levels in 17 schools participated in a project using the technique on a four hours per day, five days a week schedule with materials covered common to them all. The support of the Ministers of Education and Culture lends hope that the method may be used nationwide in the near future. At this time, however, in addition to the Bulgarian projects, Lozanov's methods are in use in Austria, Hungary, East Germany, and Russia (particularly the Academy of Pedagogical Sciences in Moscow), as well as in Canada, Japan, Columbia, France, Sweden, Norway, Denmark, Belgium, and the United States.

Suggestology in North America

The records, both verbal and written, are clear in that Dr. Jane Bancroft, Professor at Scarborough College of the University of Toronto, was the first North American educator to establish contact with Dr. Lozanov. At the encouragement of her journalist friends, Sheila Ostrander and Lynn Schroeder, who had written about Dr. Lozanov and Suggestology in their book, *Psychic Discoveries Behind the Iron Curtain*, Dr. Bancroft began a series of visits with Dr. Lozanov in 1971. Since that time, she has had occasion to continue her conferences with Dr. Lozanov at the Institute in Sofia, as well as during meetings in Bulgaria, Sweden, and in the United States. Her numerous publications concerning Suggestology and the Lozanov approach to language learning began immediately after her initial observations of the Sofia project and continue to date. Although it was not her first report in the professional literature, her article, "The Lozanov Language Class," is considered by many to be the most succinct and detailed description of suggestopedic applications to foreign language teaching and her "Suggestology and Suggestopedia: Theory of the Lozanov Method," the most thorough theoretical treatment available in the literature.

The Public Service Commission of the Canadian government sent a team of teachers under the direction of Dr. Gabriel Racle to Sofia, Bulgaria, in 1972, where they studied the theory and practice of Suggestology and Suggestopedia. They also taught French to Bulgarian students under Dr. Lozanov's supervision at the Scientific Research Institute of Suggestology. Returning to establish a pilot project in the Fall of 1972, they have implemented a language learning program which closely follows the Bulgarian model. Through adaptation of the content to meet the cultural and political exigencies of Canada, they teach French and English to monolingual Canadian civil servants in four courses, with those enrolled acquiring a higher level of functional language usage in much shorter time than through other comparable methods. Returning to Sofia annually for additional observations, they continue a clear enunciation of the application of classic Suggestology to foreign language learning.

These Canadian beginnings of applications of Suggestology are important ones. In retrospect, one would have to conclude that in the early 1970's, American psychologists and educators would have been aware of Dr. Lozanov's work and would have, in one way or another, sampled it, experimented with it, and evaluated it. This conclusion would be supported by the fact that the work of Dr. Lozanov was beginning to receive more attention and publication, and it would have entered the United States more directly if it had not been for the Canadian scholars and researchers.

The response to the knowledge of the Canadian activity in Suggestology and the gradual awareness of the professional literature concerning Suggestopedia applications, albeit not easily available nor often occurring in English, gradually created "pockets" of interest and resulted in research projects in the United States almost immediately. The places where it received attention are those which have become sufficient matters of record so that we can report them with some accuracy. They include isolated researchers, individual practitioners, and groups of individuals seeking both tests of the theory and realistic applications.

Developments in the 1970's

The first experiment utilizing the theory of Suggestology and Suggestopedia applications in the United States was in the teaching of Russian at Cleveland State College by Mariana

Kurkov in 1970. While seldom reported in the literature, she taught an experimental class in Russian using elements of Suggestopedia which had been pieced together from her professional reading. She was pleased to find that she covered twice the normal amount of content in the college level Russian course with a high level of retention on the part of her students.

During the 1971-1972 academic year, Don Schuster, Iowa State University, in much the same manner as had occurred with Mariana Kurkov, began to combine elements of his past interests in research with the reports of Suggestology and its applications to language learning. Joining with him were Ray Benitez-Bordon (who had originally called his attention to the Lozanov publications) and Charles Gritton. Their efforts, which are referred to as the Iowa Group, began with experiments with Suggestopedia applied to Spanish language learning at the college level. Although they have moved in somewhat different directions in terms of research and application, each of the three has maintained an active involvement and research interest in Suggestopedia as a specific method, as well as suggestive-accelerative activities which are related to the original Lozanov approach. Ray Benitez-Bordon has continued to refine his approach in the teaching of Spanish, with increasing rates of learning over traditionally taught college level Spanish sufficient to warrant professional publications and a high level of enthusiasm about the results. Charles Gritton, of the Des Moines Public Schools, contributed the element of the use of suggestive-accelerative activities in the teaching of mathematics and science at the junior high level. His work has not only continued, but also has been expanded to other academic areas with an emphasis on generalized applications to the public school setting. Don Schuster's many and varied research activities with the various elements of Suggestology, altering, as researchers are prone to do, independent and dependent variables, in order to determine the relative interaction of the suggestive-accelerative components, have been helpful in understanding more about the contributions of the intervening variables, as well as the end result of Suggestopedic applications.

In much the same way, Elizabeth Philipov, University of California at San Diego, was able to obtain enough information from secondary sources and from Dr. Lozanov's Bulgarian language publications to develop a dissertation concerning the use of suggestion in language learning which was completed during the 1973-1974 year. It was also due to her efforts that the First International Congress on Suggestopedia was held in Los Angeles in May of 1975, providing Dr. Lozanov an opportunity to make more American educators and researchers aware of his applications of Suggestology.

Allyn Prichard, Iowa State University, began experimental and practical applications of suggestopedic type instruction in remedial reading in Georgia public schools in the Fall of 1974, showing average gains of over 20 months on both oral and silent reading, with only 16 weeks of instruction utilizing suggestive-accelerative techniques. At Texas Tech University, Elizabeth Robinett and Lorum Stratton used a classic research design employing a control group and two experimental groups in the teaching of first-year college Spanish with Suggestopedic methods in the Spring of 1975, while colleagues began experimenting with applications in educational settings from pre-school to university class levels.

If the major clusters of interest and activity in applications of Suggestology can be located in the Iowa, Georgia, California, and Texas groups, it is because there have been individuals who were enthusiastic about the approach and were willing to give their time to continue to explore both theoretical and practical applications. Teachers in schools, in particular, have been quite receptive and willing to become involved in demonstration and pilot projects. Graduate students in their thirst for knowledge, as well as to find an approvable dissertation topic, have been strong supporters. Individuals, both in the practical applications as well as the research endeavors, who see in suggestive-accelerative techniques specific elements which can enhance learning, but which retain the involvement and dignity of the learner, as well as a positive relationship within the learning setting, have been responsive to experimentation and further investigations. Isolated and independent researchers, as well as those who come in contact with the major geographical centers for investigating suggestopedic approaches, began to make important discoveries and applications on their own. By 1976, almost all academic areas and educational levels were the subject of suggestive-accelerative projects or programs somewhere in the nation.

Two major events are worthy of identification as those which are likely to have the greatest influence and impact on the extension of suggestive-accelerative techniques, both for research and in practical settings. The most obvious is the establishment of the Society of Suggestive-Accelerative Learning and Teaching (SALT) as a vehicle to bring together the reseachers and practitioners in the field, with the *Journal of Suggestive-Accelerative Learning and Teaching* and the *SALT Newsletter* keeping interested persons informed about research and other SALT activities. A corollary and second emerging major influence is the development of the experimental teacher training program at Iowa State University and the related major research project in the Des Moines school district as a practical laboratory for testing suggestive-accelerative techniques in a school setting.

From inauspicious beginnings to auspicious activities by individuals and institutions, the approaches developed by Dr. Lozanov, and which have culminated in suggestive-accelerative applications, have moved through the nation and into all levels of the educational system. It would be conservative to say that hundreds of individuals are involved in one way or another in the research or practical application of projects which are the outgrowth of the movement, and those who have received instruction or participated in projects certainly number in the thousands. In the space of little more than five years, activity has extended from Canada to Mexico and from New York to California, with recent programs in Hawaii extending the geographical distribution even further. The Americanized version of Suggestology, while not yet come of age, is truly growing.

II.

OPERATIONAL DESCRIPTION

Suggestive-Accelerative Principles and Sequence

Suggestopedia is primarily a method to increase the capacity for memory or retention of learned material by the use of suggestion under highly favorable conditions of physical and mental relaxation. The structured and holistic setting activates the reserves of the mind, thereby more effectively utilizing the capacity which is not ordinarily employed by the individual in learning. Suggestive-accelerative learning and teaching (SALT) methodology and the resultant techniques, while not identical to Suggestopedia, follow both the philosophy and principles outlined by Lozanov as closely as possible, given the American educational setting. There are identifiable differences in the sequence and in the application of the components, but, hopefully, these practical constraints do not violate the essence of the original intent. A precise duplication of the classic Suggestopedia as developed at the Research Institute of Suggestology would, of course, be both impossible and inappropriate.

Most recently, Lozanov (1977) describes Suggestology and the Suggestopedic principles involved as: (1) a pleasant, enjoyable learning environment; (2) an absence of tension; (3) a mentally relaxed condition; (4) simultaneous use of both the conscious and unconscious; (5) a suggestive link between teacher and learner; and (6) continuous psychological feedback to the student. These principles are achieved through a Suggestopedic approach which emphasizes three conditions (Lozanov refers to them at various times both as "tools" and as "means," while Racle calls them "levels"): didactic, psychological, and artistic.

The *didactic condition* insures that the material is organized and sequential. It is presented by a trained, knowledgeable, experienced teacher in a way that meets the physical, emotional, psychological, and perceptual needs of the students. In this way, a psychotherapeutic atmosphere is maintained throughout each class period. Above all, Suggestopedic learning must bring pleasant experiences to the learner. The *psychological condition* provides an avenue to the reserves of the mind. It is perceptual, but usually subliminal, becoming the hidden curriculum which is the objective of all methodology. The psychological condition of Suggestopedia is designed to offset the finite, monotonous process of the typical classroom, which instills or replaces habits and introduces new material in an endless process of bits and pieces. Suggestopedia emphasizes a global concern, which is organized around the use of large units of material that are perceived both directly and peripherally. As such, Suggestology makes sense to the learner and the material will be learned more easily and retained longer. The *artistic condition* is achieved through the use of the arts in as many ways and as continuously as possible.

Racle (1976) lists the main principles of Suggestopedia as pseudo-passivity (mental relaxation), synthesis (combining memorization and reasoning), and suggestive interrelation (teacher/student relationship), which employ the suggestive factors of prestige, confidence (infantilization), doubleplaneness, intonation, rhythm, and concert pseudo-passivity. Bancroft (1976) indicates the principal elements are: authority, infantilization, double-planeness, intonation, rhythm, and concert pseudo-passivity. In a more recent publication, Lozanov (1977) identifies Suggestopedia as based on the three principles of joy and absence of tension, oneness of the conscious and unconscious, and suggestive interaction. While he does not identify a definitive list of components (in fact, they have changed over the years), his concern for the proper use of the elements listed by both Racle and Bancroft constitute much of the content of his speaking and writing.

Suggestive-accelerative methods, as developed in the United States since the mid-1970's, can best be described as operating within the framework of ten basic principles. All have their origins in Suggestopedic tenets. In all probability, they do not operate with equal emphasis in all SALT applications, nor would they be ordinarily ranked the same by SALT teachers. They would, however, be likely to find acknowledgment by those who have been active in teaching and research projects, at least in connection with the geographic centers of SALT activity. With some specification as to application and the right to provide some definitions of terms, both public school and adult level practitioners would tend to support the ten principles. The acceptance of the list as constituting the essence of Suggestopedia by those remaining close to the classic Lozanov method would very likely emerge as at least a modified continuum. Those whose applications have been restricted to language learning, particularly under high favorable program conditions, would probably see the list as somewhat arbitrary and perhaps in violation of some fundamental issues. Others, who have worked in diverse subject areas or under practical school conditions, might find elements of them a bit hopeful, if not idealistic.

Each of the ten principles will be covered, some in more detail than others. It should be kept in mind that they do not operate independently but are interdependent, at times to the point of making it difficult to deal with them as separate principles. The ten principles which emerge as supporting the suggestive-accelerative learning and teaching methodology are:

1. A comfortable, attractive learning setting increases acquisition and retention.
2. A relaxed state (physically and mentally) enhances learning and retention.
3. Bilateral hemisphere input into the brain (whole-brain learning) increases acquisition of new material.
4. Simultaneous use of the conscious and unconscious in learning (double-planeness) makes learning easier and more productive.
5. An organized methodology (components and sequence) overcomes the anti-suggestive barriers which reject or inhibit new learning.
6. Methodology emphasizing didactic, psychological, multi-sensory, and artistic elements increases learning and retention.
7. Enhancing of psychohygenic conditions focuses concentration, while a music background relaxes, resulting in increased recall and long-term memory.
8. Retention is increased if information is viewed as creditable and from an authoritative source.
9. A positive and encouraging learning atmosphere increases learning and retention.
10. Success in learning heightens self-concepts and promotes personal adjustment and self-confidence.

1. A Comfortable, Attractive Learning Setting Increases Acquisition and Retention.

The difficulty with the typical classroom is that the acoustics are poor and the decor is worse. Most teachers go to great lengths to relieve the drab, almost sterile, appearance which is the common stereotype of the schoolroom. While physical facilities are not as important as the general class atmosphere, they should be reasonably comfortable without external noises to detract from the effectiveness of the activities. It would be helpful if chairs and desks were separate rather than the armchair variety or bolted together as a unit. Further, if chairs or desks are fastened to the floor, it prevents both the arrangement of the room in a comfortable and relaxed setting and the provision of space for physical exercises and various group interactions. While the general classroom is more related to authority and conscious and unconscious suggestive interaction, which means that a complex of personal and physical elements are intermingled in the total evaluation of the students, the fact remains that some classroom settings have a depressing atmosphere which is difficult to offset by even the most motivated and concerned teacher. That it is often overcome by sheer teacher determination to provide a colorful, pleasant, and relaxed atmosphere in the classroom is evidenced by the fact that most individuals tend to remember *teachers* rather than classrooms.

2. A Relaxed State (Physically and Mentally) Enhances Learning and Retention.

The use of relaxation has an extensive history in medicine, psychology, psychiatry, and education. The pioneering work in the 1930's of Edmund Jacobson was based primarily on the Watsonian notion that thoughts and feelings were actually located in the peripheral musculature. Jacobson's techniques of relaxation, developed to aid people suffering from anxiety, were practiced in various forms in Europe and in this country with increasing therapeutic applications. Procedures, such as Wolpe's approach to muscle relaxation in learning settings, use electromyographic (EMG) feedback effectively. Extensive study of various types of relaxation training indicates all are effective, but the use of EMG is superior, both in speed of learning experimental recall items and depth of relaxation.

There is evidence that adults who have been taught neuromuscular relaxation techniques (by whatever method, if successful), evidence a concomitant increase in ability to handle stress and tension, ability to deal with anxiety and solve personal problems, as well as a heightened understanding of their own behavior. Both the Research Institute of Suggestology and the Canadian Public Service Commission conclude that there are individual and group psychological benefits derived by students using the Lozanov method in the specific application of language learning. These are not only the increase in feelings of confidence surrounding the learning achievement, but more specifically in the reduction of psychosomatic symptoms. Frequently mentioned in this regard are remissions of headaches, sleeplessness, anxieties, abdominal cramps, and tension; while a general improvement in personality occurs, with the individual becoming more spontaneous, creative, self-assured, and expressive.

At this point, relaxation must be classified as an older method, both for tension reduction and anxiety inhibiting objectives, but increasingly new applications and modifications are becoming more apparent in the literature. The use of relaxation as an essential element in the Wolpe model of desensitization, and the identification of the counselor as the positive reinforcement source in relaxation applications in operant conditioning, are recent cases in point. The theoretical premise that anxiety and relaxation are incompatible states of the organism leads to the conclusion that relaxation is of benefit. *What* is of benefit is still open to question.

It is likely that the relaxation itself, while an important factor, is less important than the condition created by the therapist, counselor, or teacher. A warm, understanding, sympathetic setting induces a state of mental calm which may well be more important than the muscle relaxation which is used as the vehicle in relaxation training and exercises. In fact, the evidence that it is possible to achieve muscle relaxation without reducing tension and anxiety supports the major importance of insuring relaxation in the relaxation process.

While relaxation may be related to a wide variety of learning behaviors, including evidence of enhancing retention, the most direct tie to Lozanov's theoretical position lies in the use of relaxation to circumvent the anti-suggestive barriers with its emphasis on double-planeness (conscious-unconscious unity as covered in Principle 4). While the original Suggestology experiments used muscular relaxation with specific training, recently Lozanov concluded that the suggestive atmosphere and generalized positive learning setting achieve a relaxed and alert state without emphasis on relaxation per se. One of the three major Suggestopedic principles remains, however, the absence of tension; the other two are the oneness of the conscious and unconscious, and the suggestive interaction, both of which bear direct relation to the relaxed state of the learner.

Experiments with SALT techniques in a variety of academic areas and with differing levels of learners provide evidence that relaxation is a crucial element in learning with suggestive-accelerative techniques. Results tend, in general, to parallel Lozanov's conclusion that mental relaxation is the prime characteristic, although it typically is accompanied by physical relaxation. Neither has specific training (i.e., Wolpe and Lazaraus; Jacobson) been found to be essential in the SALT applications to date. While occasional benefits (increased retention) have occurred in some projects experimenting with breathing exercises and even Yoga-type relaxation similar to Lozanov's early work, these training activities and use in daily sequences are not always deemed sufficiently enhancing to retention to warrant continuation as a part of suggestive-accelerative techniques.

Relaxation, physical and mental, is essential to SALT methodology, but it is (1) a global, almost Gestalt, learning setting atmosphere closely related to several interlocking SALT principles rather than an isolated activity; and (2) it is best achieved with a combination of learning environment characteristics rather than through specific muscle relaxation training and a daily emphasis on this segment of the suggestive-accelerative method.

Relaxation procedures, particularly those which employ suggestion in order to insure mental relaxation as well as physical or muscle relaxation, have similar objectives and follow the same generalized procedures. This is particularly true of relaxation training and techniques as proposed by writers such as Wolpe, Hartland, Lazaraus, and Wine. They all attempt, in addition to the generalized methods of relaxation, to employ a suggestive-persuasive-reeducative approach which is aimed toward increasing the self-confidence, self-understanding, and situational control of the individual or groups. While the emphasis at times in individual therapy has been on one of these aspects, it is likely that all three will be utilized in the use of relaxation as an educational technique.

Care should be exercised to avoid the confusion which frequently exists between relaxation, even when combined with suggestion, and the more specific therapeutic techniques of hypnosis or any of the popular meditation approaches. The relaxation approaches outlined here emphasize the *relaxed but alert* state of the individual, as opposed to the induced somnolent condition of hypnosis or the withdrawn state of meditation. Although hypnosis is frequently seen as heightening responsiveness to suggestion, research is inconclusive concerning its effect on learning, with recent research indicating that hypnosis may, in fact, inhibit learning efficiency. On the other hand, relaxation as an end in itself, or when combined with fantasy, has produced excellent results in a number of learning settings.

Typical classroom conditions in science, language, drama, and vocational subjects have utilized relaxation and imagery in order to increase the retention of cognitive material. In a relaxed state, for example, students visualize a scene involving the meaning of a foreign word or phrase, imagine how they would portray a dramatic scene, or—under the direction of the teacher—imagine a fantasy trip as electrons in a force field or a white corpuscle in the bloodstream.

Physical Exercises and Relaxation. Research into visual, perceptual, and motor coordination suggests that the coordination required in physical exercises and activities, such as swimming, are similar to that necessary in academic achievement, particularly learning to read. The failure to develop bilaterally is seen in communication and visual coordination difficulty, which eventually leads to reading problems. Experimental groups of children provided with special exercises, and even swimming instruction, have evidenced academic improvement sufficient to warrant efforts to provide coordination exercises on a regular basis in the early grades. Physical exercises, particularly those which result in muscle relaxation, are useful in preparation for the more general relaxation necessary in mind calming activities as well as having a more direct effect on retention. Exercises, such as found on commercial records or in teacher's manuals, as listed in the Resources section of this book, provide good starting places. Any of the familiar stretching, reaching, bending, and breathing exercises work well with most age groups. Exercises which can be done at desks or in chairs are useful when classroom limitations are encountered. Directions for selected exercises of this type will be found in the Appendix.

While physical exercises are not essential as a prerequisite to relaxation, they are useful for both general relaxation and instructional purposes. Combining exercise and learning activities (i.e., forming letters of the alphabet using the body) are particularly helpful in the lower grades. If the students have been active in the period prior to the SALT class, the exercise may be shortened or eliminated. If the students have been sitting for a long period or involved in deep concentration, such exercises are very helpful at the beginning of class. Used regularly, physical exercises can be completed in three to five minutes at the beginning of each period.

It is interesting to compare the theoretical premise of Montessori with the position of suggestive-accelerative learning in regard to exercises. The Montessori conclusion is that physical exercises as ends in themselves are of little worth, particularly the endless repetition of simplistic muscle movements. Exercises should be directed to helping in the performance of other acts, such as in normal daily activities or locomotion and speech. In fact, the Montessori position is that it is possible to educate the child's muscular sense through the refinement of exercises in ways which would create a sensory memory. This concept is akin to the principle that general refinement of movements and rhythm will generalize into a higher level of coordination, to the end that it will be lateralized into broader muscular and even academic patterns of response.

Although Lozanov indicates that muscle relaxation and breathing exercises as a pre-relaxation condition have been found to be unnecessary, since the overall relaxing and suggestive atmosphere of the class accomplishes the same thing, many SALT teachers continue to use physical exercises and muscle relaxation as a part of the daily sequence. The conclusion, of course, is that a relaxed state is essential in suggestive-accelerative methodology. Whether at a given educational level or for a specific academic area, this condition is made more likely through physical exercises leading to breathing and muscle relaxation emphasis and is one which will depend on the teacher and the conditions surrounding the class, both situationally and individually.

3. Bilateral Hemisphere Input into the Brain (Whole-Brain Learning) Increases Acquisition of New Material.

Physiologically, it could be said that we have two brains rather than one. This is not the same observation that allocates different types of functionings to the left and right brain hemispheres. The two-brain theory relates, first, to the inner, more primitive brain, which was the earliest evolved neurological structure and governs respiration, pulse rate, and blood pressure, in addition to control of some behavior patterns. The entire autonomic nervous system, and perhaps what has come to be called the "unconscious mind," are centered here. The second, topmost layer of the brain, and the latest to develop in human evolution, governs the central nervous system and is the conscious, reasoning brain containing the analytic intellect and housed in the cerebral cortex. The two brains are, of course, functionally and biologically connected in many ways which we are only now discovering and perhaps in ways we do not yet understand. Of one thing we may be sure, however; we must understand the whole brain if we understand how the modification of thoughts, feelings, sensations, emotions, attitudes, as well as intellectual and problem-solving abilities, operate in the behavior of the individual.

In addition, we have rather recently discovered that our brain's hemispheres work in two relatively independent fashions, since the left and right hemispheres of the brain have been found to have their own specialized forms of intellect. The left hemisphere is calculating, linear, and uses language, formulas, and math-like symbols. It is highly verbal and mathematical, performing with analytic, symbolic, computer-like, sequential logic. Further, it is involved in logical, analytical, linear, and sequential (especially time-bound) thought processes and specifically used in mathematical and linguistic learning.

The right hemisphere is better at visual, spatial knowledge; thinking in images and pictures; thought to be more in contact with the unconscious; and perhaps the center of what we have come to call intuition. The right, by contrast to the left, is spatial and mute, performing with a kind of information processing that cannot yet be simulated even by our most sophisticated computers. The right hemisphere is involved in creative, aesthetic, poetic, musical, artistic, simultaneous (not constrained by time), and holistic thought processes. We know that we do our best thinking and problem-solving when we integrate (coordinate) the two ways of learning, which means that in addition to our usual verbal information, we should provide experiences in visualizing the problem. Since the two hemispheres of the brain apparently can operate independently and differently, it has been assumed that one hemisphere must be dominant. Depending on the activity involved, one hemisphere will take the lead in maintaining control in order to insure coordination. Because the speech centers are almost always located in the left hemisphere, that hemisphere is usually considered to be the dominant one, while the right hemisphere has been called the minor hemisphere. (See Figure 1.)

Research into brain hemispheres indicates that the left and right hemispheres are relatively complete in themselves. Unlike animals, human brain hemispheres begin to differentiate at an early age in terms of the types of data processed and the processes themselves. For example, the left hemisphere tends to specialize in data that are important in building relationships across time. As one reads and relates each written

Figure 1

The Hemispheric Functions of the Brain

LEFT HEMISPHERE DOMINANT	RIGHT HEMISPHERE MINOR
SPEECH - VERBAL	SPATIAL - MUSICAL
Logical	Holistic
Mathematical	Artistic
Linear	Symbolic
Detailed	Simultaneous
Sequential	Emotional
Controlled	Intuitive
	Creative
Intellectual	Spiritual
Worldly	Receptive
Active	Synthesizing
Analytic	Gestalt
Critical	
Reading	Facial Recognition
Writing	Simultaneous
Naming	Comprehension
Ordering	Environmental Orientation
PERCEPTION OF SIGNIFICANT ORDER	PERCEPTION OF ABSTRACT PATTERNS

word to previous paragraphs and to all those things which have previously been committed to verbal knowledge, as well as anticipation of what will be read in the next paragraph, the left hemisphere is being used. The right hemisphere will specialize in data whose significance is from relationships perceived across space rather than time. The right hemisphere is predominant when one is orienting oneself in the surrounding environment, recognizing a face, understanding where you are in a building, or interpreting a chart or graph. The right hemisphere, therefore, has frequently been called the visual-spatial brain. The right and left hemispheres are connected by the corpus callosum and messages are transmitted from one hemisphere to the other in order to produce integrated thinking. It does *not* appear that one is born with the predisposition to use either the right or the left brain predominantly, since practice, experience, and perhaps even cultural factors may have a great deal to do with it. In like fashion, individuals who have been raised in a left brain (highly verbal, mechanically ordered) culture with practice learn to use the right brain with great facility. Without specific teaching approaches which focus on one hemisphere or the other in a problem-solving situation, a student will most likely use the one which is easiest. For example, one student will read the directions carefully and follow them sequentially in order to assemble a model, while another student will look at the configuration of the end product carefully and then put the pieces together without looking at the directions.

The three major conclusions which emerge from brain hemisphere research deal directly with how individuals learn and the efficiency with which they are taught. The first conclusion has to do with the differences in left brain and right brain functions on an individual basis. Each individual brain is, of course, truly unique in terms of temperament and talent. The second conclusion is that our educational system, and society in general, with their heavy emphasis on communication and training in the basics, or tool subjects, discriminate against one whole half of the brain. The non-verbal, non-mathematical right hemisphere has its own perceptual, mechanical, and spatial mode of apprehending and reasoning. The attention devoted in schools to right hemisphere functions is minimal compared to the amount of time which is lavished on the left hemisphere. The third and final conclusion is that we must make major changes in our idea of how the conscious mind operates in relationship to brain mechanisms. The long established materialistic and behavioristic thinking as the major, if not only, way in which knowledge, understanding, insight, and perspectives can be assimilated into usable intelligence must give way to the fact that the right hemisphere can make important contributions to education.

The recent concern for the lack of right hemisphere development, particularly due to the left hemisphere emphasis in most educational methodology, has resulted in a number of suggestions to schools and teachers. If schools are to provide optimum cognitive opportunities for children to develop, it will necessitate additional types of experiences and modification of some methodologies. In a more general vein, it has been observed that the typical classroom rigidity needs to be relaxed, with teachers accepting responses from students which are not always specific and sequential. Permitting, if not encouraging, children to use their intuition and express general ideas and hunches as opposed to specific content would be a way to move in such directions.

Teachers have emphasized listening skills more in recent years, and this should provide important right hemisphere activity. Despite the crowded daily class schedule, teachers may need to provide more waiting time for responses from students, particularly those who are not as left hemisphere oriented. While it seems to be somewhat in opposition to the emphasis on the scientific process and objectivity, students may need to be encouraged to base conclusions on and to risk verbalizing solutions without supporting observable evidence in a number of cases. The "educated guess" may have an important contribution to make in many classrooms. Imagination and even creativity would be enhanced thereby. The emphasis on whole-brain learning adds yet another argument against the excessive use of rote learning and repetitive practice in teaching methodology.

It would, of course, be desirable for teachers to present information simultaneously to both hemispheres, something that good teachers have perhaps always done. Using charts, graphs, or even diagramming on the chalkboard while presenting a verbal explanation is a case in point. Under some conditions, it will be better to direct teaching to each hemisphere in sequence. When students read materials followed by preparing charts, diagrams, or drawings; or when they develop maps followed by a verbal presentation of information contained on the map, this procedure would be followed. More use of music, poetry, art, and visual components in all teaching areas and activities would do much to encourage right hemisphere learning and augment left hemisphere stimulation.

The point is that most of what happens in school has been primarily through a left hemisphere input of reading and listening and a left hemisphere output of talking and writing systems which have failed to utilize the tremendous creative and learning capacity which is contained in the right hemisphere. Fortunately, we now have a better understanding of the learning processes of the two hemispheres, and, in addition, we are beginning to develop tools, techniques, methods, and materials which will emphasize whole-brain learning and the bilateral input into both hemispheres, which can accelerate the learning process and insure longer retention of the material which has been learned by students at all levels. Teachers are encouraged to become familiar with some of the basic and most interesting commentaries concerning whole-brain learning that have appeared recently. Especially recommended are Brandwein and Ornstein (1977), Buzan (1976), Ferguson (1973), Galin (1976), Hunter (1976), Rennels (1976), Samples (1975, 1977), and Tart (1975). Additional references relating to subject matter applications will be found in the Resources section of this book.

There are those who speculate that the explanation of the decline in school achievement in recent years is due to the fragmented and specialized learning process required in the typical school curriculum. The isolation of subject areas, specificity of learning activities, almost total emphasis on left hemisphere language involvement, and diminishing concern for the total learning atmosphere have resulted in a lack of involvement and, at times, hope for both student and teacher alike. Higher levels of achievement in the past could be said to have resulted from a learning setting which was more attentive to the whole child, used a wide variety of sensory inputs, and evidenced a more positive relationship between the teacher and learner. Such conclusions are difficult to substantiate and may not be accurate. There is no doubt, however, that there is an unbalanced emphasis on left brain activities and left hemisphere involvement in the curriculum and methods of the school. A reduction of left brain language emphasis may not be either possible or desirable, since an increased emphasis on right hemisphere functions would be more helpful to the educational development of the student. There is need, at least, to balance the learning input which constitutes the day-to-day curriculum content with emphasis on the sensory, spatial, and creative processes of the right hemisphere in order to achieve a balance in the educational system. In the process, learning should be enhanced, and, if some critics are correct, a measurable increase in achievement will be evidenced in the future. Suggestive-accelerative learning techniques—with their emphasis on creative imagery, music background component, and general holistic, multisensory emphasis—can provide immeasurable help in this direction.

4. Simultaneous Use of the Conscious and Unconscious in Learning (Double-Planeness) Makes Learning Easier and More Productive.

Double-planeness (conscious and unconscious) is the principle which taps the little-used portion of the individual's abilities in learning. Suggestive-accelerative techniques must activate the unconscious as well as the conscious if rapid learning is to take place. The communicative act involving verbal and non-verbal signals insures that this occurs. There is need, of course, for both the conscious and verbal and the unconscious and non-verbal to be consistent. Words, gestures, and facial expressions must convey an air of sincerity, dedication, warmth, and acceptance, as well as establish an authoritative identity for the teacher. In the same vein, intonation carries both a conscious element and has a suggestive influence on the unconscious mental activity. Communication researchers have concluded that over half a message is conveyed through non-verbal means.

The teacher conveys a certainty and confidence as well as creating a positive (and suggestive) atmosphere in much the same way an actor projects a character in both obvious and intangible ways. It is through double-planeness that Lozanov believes one may call upon the non-specific mental reactivity, which is where the unused learning capacity lies. He has variously used estimates of 90 percent to 95 percent as the amount of this unused potential. Whatever the amount, there is little question that individuals typically operate far below their ability level in learning. Suggestive-accelerative techniques and the resultant atmosphere attacking both the conscious (verbal) and unconscious (non-verbal) planes of communication help students more nearly approach their learning capacities.

5. An Organized Methodology (Components and Sequence) Overcomes the Anti-Suggestive Barriers Which Reject or Inhibit New Learning.

Lozanov's methods combine memory expansion and relaxation, creating an alert but relaxed state of mind, during which the anti-suggestive barriers are lowered and there is an increasing receptiveness of the individual to suggestion and retention of new information. He hypothesizes that everyone is continually exposed to suggestion from the environment. In order to protect oneself from receiving too much stimuli, anti-suggestion barriers are established. The three anti-suggestion barriers are: first, the critical-logical barrier, which rejects all that does not make a logical impression; the intuitive-affective barrier, which rejects all that does not create a feeling of confidence and security; and the moral-ethical barrier, which rejects all that contradicts the principles and values of the individual. In bypassing the defense mechanisms, it is possible to reach the unused 90 percent of the brain with a resultant increased learning speed and retention of material. More important, this occurs with very little effort on the part of the individual. Relaxation techniques and deep breathing exercises are used in order to reduce anxiety, free the mind of distractions which hamper learning, and allow the new material to be more easily received and retained. Lozanov theorizes that much of the difficulty in retaining new material can be attributed to the fact that it must compete with old or existing material and that in the relaxed state this condition is alleviated to a great extent. The role of music is to support the learning process by acting as a medium to activate the subconscious. In effect, by being in a relaxed and tranquil state augmented by a musical background, there can be a direct flow of information to the unconscious regions. This results in automatically assimilating the material with speed and economy of effort that is not possible under any other learning conditions. In addition, theoretically, language input into the right hemisphere of the brain is possible only if it is accompanied by music or uses a rhythmic or poetic mode. The musical background and rhythmic repetition of material in Suggestopedia provide for the language content to be lateralized in the left hemisphere and also to be coded in the right hemisphere.

In the overcoming of the anti-suggestive barriers, or as Lozanov more recently refers to it, the desuggestive-suggestive factors, it is essential to activate the reserves of the learner's ability to learn—and retain—information. As with other elements, this component cannot be carried out in isolation but only in combination with other important factors. The extension of SALT techniques carries out the emphasis on the suggestive influence, integrated into the whole, and as a specific, continuing part of suggestive-accelerative activities. The objective is to remove the anti-suggestive barriers by using every avenue to reduce or circumvent them. Care must be taken to approach the students in ways to counter each of the anti-suggestive barriers.

For most students, a long and consistent history of building the critical-logical barrier exists. Typically, the interpretations of significant others, teachers, and eventually internalized self-evaluation are to the effect that very few people have high ability and learn with ease. That learning can be easy and effortless, particularly for oneself, is difficult to believe.

Such observations are new and strange, make little sense, and apparently fly in the face of all the individual's prior knowledge about learning. An educational history of grades, evaluations, and reports, frequently negative in nature, have served to reinforce these beliefs. Teachers using suggestive-accelerative techniques make special efforts at the outset to present the method as an effective and successful approach to effortless learning. The positive and authoritative position is an important beginning point and is maintained throughout by continual reference to the fact that learning will be greater than ever experienced before. Early on, ungraded tests verify the fact that learning is taking place under the method, and this further serves to counter the critical-logical barrier.

The intuitive-affective barrier is erected throughout the life of the person. Every failure which has been identified and emphasized serves to establish a negative feeling and to lower self-esteem. In the end, it is much easier (and seems more accurate) to conclude that one will have difficulty learning and will be more likely to fail than succeed. Any learning task, therefore, will be met with the immediate reaction of, if not negative, typically a low evaluation of one's ability to learn. The teacher needs to work very hard in overcoming the ingrained feeling of insecurity which is felt (affectively) and displayed automatically (intuitively) whenever a learning setting is encountered. Showing confidence in the student's ability as well as a positive regard for the student as a capable person must be a constant part of the teacher-student interaction. With evidence of success, it becomes easier to overcome the intuitive-affective barrier. The teacher, however, uses every opportunity to demonstrate a high level of confidence in, as well as a positive personal regard for, the student's ability. Such attitudes are a critical part of suggestive-accelerative learning.

Past experience in learning tasks has resulted in most students concluding that learning is hard work, but that it *must be so* in order to be worthwhile. Society has continually indicated that personal, economic, and even religious values of work are centered in sacrifice and dedication, even to the point of drudgery. To find enjoyment in working and learning and even joy in the tasks is in direct opposition to the moral-ethical barrier. Teachers need to emphasize that effort can be expended in a pleasant and enjoyable learning activity and that the results will be equal to or exceed those which occur when one must force the learning effort. Part of the circumvention of this barrier comes in the fact that suggestive-accelerative methods are usually fun for learners. When, in addition, they find that retention is better than before, it becomes easier to offset the expectation that learning must be unpleasant to be effective.

The anti-suggestive barriers exist in an interrelated way, and quite likely cannot be offset in isolated fashion. Figure 2 gives a diagrammatical illustration of how they may operate in blocking out positive suggestions. The diagram (modified from one proposed by Dr. Allyn Pritchard) indicates that the critical-logical barrier is essentially at the conscious level, while the intuitive-affective and moral-ethical barriers operate at both the conscious and unconscious levels. The need for double-planeness (conscious and unconscious) aspects of instruction is clearly in evidence.

If, as postulated, the anti-suggestive barriers are erected over time by the individual's interaction with the environment, they become internalized for reasons of personal feelings of security and to protect the self from the onslaught of critical, devaluating evidence which implies limits of ability and capacity. Once established, they are more likely to be reinforced than diminished. At the least, they become convenient filters which make interaction easier, but limit hope and aspiration. If positive suggestions make an impact, they

Figure 2

Anti-Suggestive Barriers

Critical-logical barrier: intelligence and beliefs
Intuitive-affective barrier: confidence and security
Moral-ethical barrier: values and principles

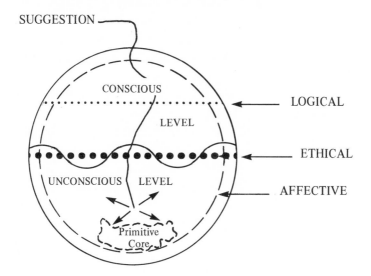

Suggestion must comply with requirements of each barrier if it is accepted.

Barriers maintained for protection, security, maintenance, convenience.

Avenues or channels around barriers:
    teacher's verbal communication
    teacher's non-verbal communication
    student's peer influences
    instructional materials
    classroom learning setting
    student's auto-suggestion
    instructional methodology (SALT)

must first survive the blocking of the barriers. It is important, therefore, to utilize all available avenues to offsetting the barriers (i.e., desuggestion). The role of the teacher as a knowledgeable, trusted individual is, of course, a major factor. It is important in this regard that the total communicative act (which is really what a suggestive-accelerative setting is all about) be consistent. The teacher's verbal and nonverbal communication is in itself a double-plane feature of the class. In addition, peer influences will be felt, hopefully in positive ways, with the observation that all students are learning and having fun. The instructional materials, setting, and methodology all play a part. What the teacher does and how it is done contribute to the acceptance of suggestion by the student. Finally, as success is evidenced, the student will begin to believe more in himself or herself, and it becomes easier to circumvent the anti-suggestive barriers with positive, enhancing suggestions regarding the learning process as well as the individual's performance.

The positive results from suggestive-accelerative techniques may be explained, at least in part, by the theoretical premise that memory (retention) is a result of context or background rather than association, which has been the historic explanation. In relating this interpretation to suggestive-accelerative learning, Schuster *et al.* (1976) point out that contextualism explains things from the top down, which is consistent with the global nature of SALT teaching, while the older associationist, from the bottom up interpretation, served well for independent word memory. The total environmental interaction of suggestive-accelerative methodology, resulting from an organized and sequential approach, overcomes the anti-suggestive barriers and provides a relational structure which aids both learning and retention.

6. Methodology Emphasizing Didactic, Psychological, Multi-Sensory, and Artistic Elements Increases Learning and Retention.

From Dewey to the most current application of Piaget, it is concluded that the child acts on the environment and that what the environment is like determines whether cognitive processes will be delayed or enhanced. The child acts on the environment through physical and sensory interaction, experimenting with objects, and experiencing persons and setting. For the classroom, however, the role of methodology is to avoid leaving the environment to chance. The teacher, regardless of philosophical inclination or theoretical beliefs, will devise structure, plan activities, organize experiences, provide equipment, and have at least some notion, if not exhaustive lists, of what objectives of learning are involved and how they may be evaluated for the appropriate developmental level of the child. Hopefully, all teachers strive to create a rich classroom learning environment and to provide a structure in keeping with the child's stage of development. While the structure is more evident in dealing with the agreed-upon lists of skills to be accomplished at each developmental stage, there is an underlying expectation that the development of self, as well as social-emotional development, will be a natural and concomitant result.

The research evidence generally indicated that unless a child receives adequate sensory experience, it will become difficult to deal efficiently with later learning activities. Of course, for the very young child, the processing of information is essentially related to the development of sensory perception. The interpretation of our environment and our experiences is a learned activity beginning in infancy and accelerating during the early years, and is the basic ingredient in concept formation.

Learning is dependent on the capacity to use multi-sensory

input for greatest effectiveness. Obviously, much learning occurs without total sensory involvement, but it is made more difficult thereby. For children, the use of visual and auditory perception in a coordinated way is particularly important. Educational materials, by and large, deal at most with perceptual-motor training, with little regard for the role of the hemispheres of the brain. Historically, this limitation is understandable due to the complexity of hemispheric brain functions and the lack of a useful theoretical premise relating brain hemispheres to learning. Much of the brain research has dealt with highly specific functions or biological analysis which has not been brought together in a way which can be used to understand the learning act as a whole-brain interaction.

Suggestive-accelerative learning emphasizes a concentrated use of the arts in all their multi-sensory dimensions. This is done, not from the pleasure that the arts bring, although certainly there is pleasure for most learners in art, music, graphics, poetry, and dramatic presentations, but rather for the right hemispheric emphasis and the overall relaxation the arts provide. The music background and the nature of the concert session serve to accomplish much of this objective. The artistic condition does not mean a renewed emphasis on the active, dramatic presentation of material, which has largely been replaced by a second concert session by Lozanov (although the Canadian language program appears to retain this presentation and many SALT teachers feel it is an important element in the method). The artistic condition is met through a concentrated influence of the arts and is totally integrated into the learning process.

7. *Enhancing of Psychohygenic Conditions Focuses Concentration, While a Music Background Relaxes, Resulting in Increased Recall and Long-Term Memory.*

The music background in suggestive-accelerative learning is an important element from several standpoints. As a part of the total conscious-unconscious duality of the learning setting, it contributes to the non-specific mental activity which activates the reserves of the mind. Music reaches the unconscious easily and evokes feelings which can be used, not only in a general atmosphere setting role, but also in conveying content or emphasizing elements of the material to be learned. The music and rhythm, if correctly selected, also have a direct relaxing effect. While Lozanov concludes that the music is, in the final analysis, a placebo and that the same relaxed setting can be brought about by the instructor's general interaction with the class, the fact remains that for many classes the music is a more expedient and significant relaxing agent.

Music and rhythm also play an important role in the bilateral input of material into both hemispheres of the brain. The music, as a carrier, aids in the lateralization of the content in the right hemisphere, thus enhancing memory and recall. While rhythm alone can accomplish the right hemisphere augmentation, and some SALT teachers prefer this approach, much of the academic subject matter taught in schools would be difficult to convert to a precise rhythmic presentation. The combination of rhythm, intonation, rhyming, and music make for a four-fold emphasis on bilateral input which is possible in language learning (and perhaps a few other areas), but would be even more difficult to achieve for most academic areas. Some SALT projects have used a metronome to insure the rhythm sequence is matched to the music, while Lozanov has secured the talents of noted Bulgarian composers in writing special music to accompany sections of material to be taught.

Finally, there is the value of music as a cultural, creative, and dramatic art form which provides an important experience for the learner apart from the relaxing and retention enhancing qualities. Lozanov feels quite strongly about the use of classical music, not only because of the nature of the relaxation which is induced by classical music, but also because of the aesthetic benefits which may be derived. He reports that elementary school children are interested in classical music and that they develop a love for it as a result of hearing it in the background during their class periods. He also indicates that adults who have not been exposed to classical music develop an interest in the opera and in concerts as a result of their experience with music as a background for therapy or learning. Some SALT teachers have received comments from the young adults in their programs that they find the classical music monotonous, but this has usually resulted from using a single selection for an extended period on a daily basis. In some research projects, students have expressed an interest in a greater variety of music, which can usually be accommodated without violating the basic purpose of the music background. Appropriate background music for children may be a larger problem, although it appears that classical music is the best available at this time for most purposes.

It appears that large ranges of types and instrumentation in music can be used effectively as background, as long as it does not violate some general principles of tempo and loudness. Certainly, no music background should intrude to the extent that it overpowers. Neither should it invoke sleep nor stimulate the student to the detriment of learning the material which is being introduced. In a general way, any intrusive element of the music becomes counterproductive. Finding appropriate background music, therefore, does take effort on the part of the teacher. Experience has shown, however, that the latitude is wider than first imagined. Some SALT teachers even use local FM music stations on a daily basis without difficulty. The major problems arise from using background music for which the words (even though the lyrics are not a part of the performance) are well-known to the students. This familiarity seems to create a type of intrusion of its own. As might be expected, the greatest problem has been found to reside in students who are musicians, particularly instrumentalists. They attend to the music in such a manner as to interfere with the input of content. Their attention is focused on the technique, style, and articulation of the performer (in the case of a single instrument) or on the interpretation of a group. Frequently, they are moved in their imagery and thoughts to past performances or experiences which command their total attention.

Thinking about, or attending to, the music in a peaceful, restful manner allows the music to be the carrier for material to be lateralized in both hemispheres of the brain. Music serves as an agent of relaxation which enhances the capacity to learn new material and increases recall for the material. In its own way, music backgrounds provide a cultural and artistic experience which is enriching for the student. Music backgrounds, therefore, while not essential if other suggestive-accelerative factors are maintained, does become an important adjunct to learning and one which most SALT teachers would judge high on the list of suggestive-accelerative components.

8. Retention Is Increased if Information Is Viewed as Creditable and From an Authoritative Source.

While the prestige and authority of the teacher are important suggestive factors in desuggestion, or overcoming anti-suggestive barriers, they are equally important in establishing the total learning climate. Although the immediate evaluation by the student in this regard will center on the teacher, the institution itself, methodology, materials, and the classroom setting will contribute to the confidence the student has in learning. Directly related to the authority of the teacher (and the combined environment) is the response of the learner as spontaneous and confident. In many ways, the student has a child-like trust and belief in the teacher and system. This is particularly so in activities which involve songs, games, and role playing. Unfortunately, Lozanov refers to this tendency as infantilization—unfortunate, in that it may be confused with Freudian theory or age regression rather than as an attempt to identify the more general receptivity of children who are calm, yet eager to learn.

Rhythm and voice intonation are best considered together, particularly during the presentation of new material during the concert session. Memorization is most effective when the material is conveyed to the student in a rhythmical manner and in varied voice levels during the repetition stage. Three presentations, using three intonations and voice levels, rhythmically orchestrated to the music with consideration for the spacing, pauses, and amplitude more nearly insure bilateral input into both hemispheres of the brain. Such presentation, however, for much subject matter material would be extremely difficult. To prepare academic material in this manner would undoubtedly be a time-consuming and expensive matter, possible only in special research or project conditions and not likely to occur in practical school settings.

The three intonations, which used either in presenting the material three times (triads) or in sequencing material presented once or twice, require the teacher to present the first word, phrase, or passage in a calm, confident, declarative, but essentially normal voice. The next presentation would be a whispered but clear and quiet tone with a softness of the voice. This almost subliminal presentation not only provides a variation which is helpful in attending but which also has been found to enhance the retention of material. In earlier experiments, Lozanov demonstrated the effective use of a "whisper method" for both language learning and psychotherapy. Whether the quiet intonation provides a link with the unconscious mental activity or if the variation is primarily important from the attention the contrast provides, the use of the quiet voice in presentation is an element in suggestive-accelerative methodology which is incorporated whenever possible.

The third presentation is one which is an authoritative, loud, commanding tone. This latter pronunciation is in keeping with the authoritative principle of suggestive-accelerative learning which implies the suggestive nature of the tonal quality and conveys an atmosphere of confidence. The three presentations in distinct intonations accomplish the need for repetition without the boring and deadening effects of monotony. The variations, first in a normal or declaratory tone of voice, the second in a soft whisper, and the third in a commanding tone provide the straightforward, subtle, and authoritative presentations which accomplish the need for variety and contrast, but also fulfill the theoretical basis for suggestive-accelerative learning.

9. A Positive and Encouraging Learning Atmosphere Increases Learning and Retention.

The teacher who is liked and respected is one who creates a positive learning climate, at times without knowing precisely what the conditions are which have resulted in the desirable setting. The physical and social setting of the classroom, including the conscious and unconscious signals, are more important in the attitude, discipline, and achievement of the student than the content, method, or techniques used by the teacher. The recent emphasis on the teacher as "instrument" rather than "source" may convey the same concern for the teaching-learning process.

It is difficult to separate the principle of a positive and encouraging class atmosphere from a number of closely related principles of suggestive-accelerative learning. Such an atmosphere depends on many things, but primarily it is determined by the teacher's own attitude. The handling of the desuggestive barriers (covered in an earlier section), the knowledgeable and authoritative presentation, and other factors all contribute to the expectation that learning will take place in a pleasant, easy manner. Part of the encouraging atmosphere is conveyed by the structure of method. Another helpful factor is the use of control or check quizzes which are graded by the student and not seen by the teacher, particularly in the early stages of presenting new material. A positive approach to learning must be substantiated by results on the part of the learner if it is to continue to be effective—or even believed. The conscious and unconscious (double-planeness) communication is also at issue here. As pointed out in other applications of suggestive-accelerative principles, the constant and consistent coincidence of verbal and non-verbal communication is essential.

The choice of words to introduce both the method and each daily presentation of material must be done with care. The positive atmosphere must avoid references, even oblique ones, which might convey to the learner that the material will be difficult or that great effort will be required to learn. This becomes a difficult assignment for teachers more attuned to admonishments regarding the need to pay attention, work hard, and expend every effort if they expect to succeed (i.e., learn, repeat, and make high marks). Evaluation does take place, but only *after* students have seen evidence that they are learning under the system and have experienced what, by prior standards, is effortless learning. Evaluation also calls for a greater variety of appraisal techniques than frequently used, or at least a different type. The use of group activities through presentations, demonstrations, and performances can be used by the teacher as adjuncts to the more typical comprehensive essay and objective tests. In some areas, a practical demonstration or application either in the classroom or outside the school is a better indication of learning and may be an effective check on achievement. Such appraisal techniques may be more easily applied to some academic areas than to others (language learning, for example), but with care and planning their use should be possible for teachers of many subjects at all levels.

The positive setting is maintained through a variety of activities during the presentation of material. The use of games, songs, role playing, dramatic presentations, field trips, and other activities which are interesting as well as educational have the advantage of being closer to the life of the student and the application of the material which is presented. Transfer, by whatever definitions are used, is thereby enhanced for each student. That these learning experiences are enjoyable is a criterion, as it should be regardless of the material or method used by the teacher. In language learning and some other areas, the students are given a new identity, including name and biography, to even further remove the negative effects of errors. In effect, the student is able to participate in class as another person, both imaginatively and in class interaction, thus reducing concern for mistakes and making learning a pleasant activity. Above all, mistakes should be corrected in a non-threatening manner which avoids criticism or embarrassment.

The acceptance of the student as an individual and providing a pleasant class setting may involve doing extra or special things, some of which are a part of many teachers' approaches. At times it seems to be going to extremes, such as when text material is introduced into the language class of Lozanov. Students use no text or written materials for the first week, after which they are presented in a special ceremony with flowers and a card for each student. One is reminded, however, of the ceremonies which accompany the routine events of a classroom during the early years; ceremonies which say to the student that learning and their presence is something special. It is interesting how such activities gradually diminish over the years as school attendance progresses (and, conversely, as joy in learning usually decreases).

Probably all of the suggestive-accelerative components are designed to communicate the pleasure of learning and the importance of the student as an individual. Since this element is of central importance, it becomes not only an overall attitude but a principle which deserves special attention on a day-to-day basis by the teacher.

10. Success in Learning Heightens Self-Concepts and Promotes Personal Adjustment and Self-Confidence.

Both Suggestology and Suggestopedia make use of the positive and encouraging atmosphere not unlike that emphasized in all helping professions. In addition, however, the teacher must maintain a position of knowledgeable authority on one hand and the ability to develop a sympathetic understanding with students on the other. It is believed that one remembers best those things which come from an authoritative source; thus, one of the repetitions used in the triad includes reinforcement in an authoritative tone. It is also important that students have confidence in their own ability and in the success of the teaching method. As such, a positive atmosphere and inspirational statements are frequently incorporated in the relaxation and suggestive sequences. Students are encouraged and complimented in a positive and hopeful manner. If mistakes are made, they are corrected, but in a quiet and non-critical way.

Much of the outcome of suggestive-accelerative learning is in terms of personal adjustment. At all levels, Lozanov indicates that individuals who have participated in Suggestopedic projects have increased their self-concepts and have emerged with a changed attitude about themselves. Essentially, he feels that individuals, through past learning, have experienced difficulty in assimilating positive and helpful suggestions and have become discouraged and doubtful of their own abilities. One of the Suggestopedic techniques is to have individuals repeat positive statements and suggestions to themselves in an overall atmosphere of positive encouragement. At times, this technique is a part of the relaxation sequence in suggestive-accelerative methodology. All suggestive-accelerative components use a hopeful, encouraging approach to students, although it varies from direct suggestions and overt compliments to the presence of a warm, encouraging atmosphere which conveys the support rather than the use of words.

Research over several decades has consistently pointed out that there exists a positive relationship between self-concept and achievement in school. Much of society teaches self-degradation rather than building self-esteem as children grow and develop. The end result is that children accept the more negative view of themselves and, in addition, add their own negative self-referent feelings and evaluations.

If self-confidence resides in belonging, competence, and self-worth, suggestive-accelerative methods have direct implications for the value placed on the self by the student. The whole class atmosphere is one in which the student is seen as important and accepted. The central theme of the method is that learning will take place and there is continued assurance that they will succeed as described. When students have evidence that they have learned with greater ease, their view of themselves as capable persons enhances the value they place on their own worth.

Suggestive-Accelerative Sequence

To describe a typical suggestive-accelerative class, except in the most general way, would be difficult. Even descriptions of the classes in language learning held at the Institute in Sofia vary with the observers and over the years. This is partly attributed to the degree of involvement by those who have visited or been trained by Lozanov and his staff, as well as an obvious selective perception which operates with individual observers. It would be more accurate, however, to attribute the major portion of the variance to the historical development of the system. In the early development (pre-1970) years, a number of elements and emphases occurred which were subsequently eliminated or deemphasized. Even the current (late 1970's) pattern may well continue the history of modification. There was—and is—sufficient evidence that the method represents a unique combination of elements and an emphasis on sequence which can be regarded as an original contribution to education. Certainly it warrants continued evaluation and application of both the ideas on which it is based and the components which make up the whole.

The physical facilities of the Institute are designed specifically for implementation of the Lozanov method, and may be considered as a standard, if not ideal. The desirable class size is 12, with recliner lounge chairs with a swing-away type desk arm arranged in a semi-circle facing the teacher. The rooms are relatively small in keeping with the smaller class size, with two loud speakers located on the front wall and a small stage area in one corner which is used for role playing and dramatic presentations. A conveniently placed television set, which can be used for the presentation of material and for closed circuit viewing of presentations of other classes, is available. The recliner chairs are particularly useful during relaxation and the concert session of the presentation, while versatile and technically advanced audio-visual equipment is available to augment the presentations. American projects have not been so technically fortunate. Many experiments have been carried out in standard classrooms with typical furniture and with the use of school-type audio-visual equipment. The fact that promising results and significant increases in learning occurred even under those almost drastically different circumstances is testimony to the method as opposed to the physical setting. While ideal facilities are always an objective, using what one has available in an effective manner is possible with the suggestive-accelerative techniques.

The length of the Lozanov class is not based only on the fact that language learning was the original subject matter. For language learning, and perhaps other areas as well, it was concluded that intensive daily sessions produce more learning than shorter periods over an extended time. The problems of fatigue and boredom which usually accompany extended learning sessions are avoided by the relaxed condition of the student and the interaction of other Suggestopedic components. Probably something could be said also for the highly motivated adult learners who constituted the majority of the students in the Institute's language classes. The majority of American suggestive-accelerative projects have not been developed with such intensive time frames, even in language learning. In schools and colleges for the most part, the typical 40-50 minute school period is, of necessity, the class time allotment. In working with younger children, some suggestive-accelerative activities of 10-30 minutes duration have been designed. This is particularly true in teaching early concept and language acquisition skills in early childhood education.

The same general comparisons are true for class size. Lozanov's work with Bulgarian public schools now involves larger groups than his original experiments, but there is no doubt that he prefers the smaller classes. Class size groups in American projects have depended on assignments of pupils rather than selection. Classes in early childhood education, organized around grouping and with multiple teachers or aides and frequently in open concept settings, can arrange to work with small groups of eight to ten students. Typically, classes in upper grades must adjust to 20-30 students or more. At the college level, some classes have numbered over 50. Most of the research in the literature have used classes as they existed in the organization of the school setting. Few have been devised by selecting small groups of special students. In terms of applicability and replication, this has been a desirable circumstance. Suggestive-accelerative methods can be adapted to typical school settings and realistic educational conditions—and still they show evidence of considerable benefit for the students involved. This is a convincing argument in favor of further application of the techniques.

The sequence of Suggestopedia presents problems similar to the ones encountered in defining the setting. Changes in sequence in the Institute over time and differences in observers' reports make an all-inclusive statement difficult, and, in all probability, inaccurate. The sequence used in the Canadian program is quite likely the one most nearly representative of the classic approach. Detailed analysis of either would, however, be of little worth to the majority of those interested in applying suggestive-accelerative techniques, since they are designed for language learning and utilize the extended time span. The Americanized versions of Suggestopedia have concentrated on sequence which is in keeping with the component structure of the method and allows modification appropriate to the age level, subject area, and practical school settings.

While there is obviously some abbreviation of the sequence in the shorter time span used with younger students or for highly specific topics, the general presentation emphasizes three elements. The first phase provides preparation for the material through exercises, relaxation, mind calming, and general positive suggestion. The second phase actively presents material in a multi-sensory input fashion, using dramatic, creative presentations. The third phase is the passive or concert session set to a music background and using the rhythmic and intonation emphases which are techniques designed to enhance learning and increase recall.

More specifically, the suggestive-accelerative method could be posed as a 12-step sequence. These include:

1. *Learning Setting*: attractive decor, aesthetically pleasing, comfortable, music background.

2. *Positive Atmosphere*: positive suggestions, efficient class organization, emphasis on learning as easy and fun.

3. *Physical Exercises*: helpful physical relaxation activities.

4. *Relaxation Exercises*: activities prelude to mind calming.

5. *Mind Calming*: activities prelude to concentration.

6. *Positive Suggestion*: suggestion specific to the lesson or material, suggestion to group and individual learner.

7. *Review of Prior Material*: review in traditional or innovative manner, individualized or group oriented.

8. *Preview of New Material*: preview of what is to be learned, outline of new material to be presented.

9. *Active Presentation*: material presented in dramatic, artistic, creative way, emphasizing imagery.

10. *Passive Presentation*: material presented in subtle, quiet intra-active manner.

11. *Practice*: student involvement, active discussion or response, student interaction.
12. *Close*: brief review, discussion, applications, content checks, evaluation.

The above sequence is adjusted depending on a number of factors. For example, the use of physical exercises is based not only on personal preference and the planned presentation, but also the current activities of the class. Students, particularly young children, who have been quiet and sedentary for some time before the class (watching a 45-minute movie, for example), may well need a number of physical exercises prior to relaxation and concentration. By contrast, those returning from a lunch period, the playground, or a physical education class would benefit more from moving directly into the relaxing and mind calming exercises. The same observations would hold for other steps in the sequence. In the final analysis, the teacher will be the best judge of what sequences to emphasize and which ones to minimize or eliminate, based on knowledge of the students, school conditions, and the material to be presented in a suggestive-accelerative approach.

Schuster *et al.* (1976) propose the following sequence for the programs which have been supervised by the Iowa group. Their work has been primarily with junior high and above age groups but has been carried out in a number of academic areas. With some modification, the sequence should serve a wide range of applications.

    I. Preliminary Preparation
        A. Suggestive Positive Atmosphere
            1. Desuggestive Barriers Circumvention
            2. Positive Suggestions
            3. Control Quiz Expectations
        B. Student Preparation
            1. Physical Relaxation

      2. Mind Calming
      3. Early Pleasant Learning Restimulation
    C. Lesson Planning
      1. Motivational Objectives
      2. Style (Methods and Materials)
      3. Unit Content
      4. Music Background
II. Presentation of Material
    A. Review of Previous Material
    B. Active Presentation of New Material
      1. Dynamic Presentation
      2. Imagery Association
      3. Multi-Sensory Experiencing
    C. Passive Concert Phase
      1. Breathing Synchronization
      2. Orchestrated Material
      3. Mind Calming
III. Practice
    A. Active Involvement (Lab, Group Activities)
    B. Control Quizzes
    C. Evaluation and Appraisal

Racle (1976) has presented a sequence of language courses in the classic Suggestopedic format. His outline, however, is for the five-week course and there is no detailed information concerning the sequence within each day's activities, which are three-hour instruction sections. He does identify some of the components which are used during the daily sequence of dialogues, providing a good understanding of content and activities in a general way.

Dean Held has carried out a number of suggestive-accelerative projects in Wisconsin. His major area of research and concentration is the teaching of reading. The daily lesson sequence which he proposes and the one he uses in teacher training classes includes the major components in the following order:

A. *Preparation Phase*
  1. Relaxation
  2. Mind Calming
  3. Suggestion
B. *Active Session*
  1. Multi-Sensory Activity
  2. Drama
  3. Creative Activity
  4. Language Experience
C. *Passive Session*
  1. Pseudo-Passive Activity
  2. Auditory Only
  3. Music
  4. Rhythm
  5. Intonation
  6. Creative Presentation

In the typical 50-minute class found at the secondary and college levels, the class sequence shown in Figure 3 has been used for a number of academic areas, including English, Languages, Accounting, and Business Management, as well as the sequence for SALT units in other courses or projects.

Suggestive-accelerative methods are usually identified as providing a unique combination of components, which, when used in a total classroom environment, promote learning and retention. While the components may be summarized in rather general ways or broken down into almost innumerable sub-categories, the major components involved in the learning sequence and which are a part of the basic principles described in the previous section would include 14 principal elements.

  1. Aesthetic Setting
  2. Encouraging Atmosphere

Figure 3

Daily Class Schedule (50-Minute Class)

Time Elapsed

0-20	Review of Old Material —Regular class activities, including discussion, exercises, tests, group activities, questions, and answers.
20-27	Preparation
(20-22)	—(Physical Exercise if appropriate)
20-24	—Relaxation Exercise
24-27	—Mind Calming
27-48	Presentation of New Material
27-34	—First Presentation—External/Active/Relaxed (Straightforward presentation with instructional materials and/or outer references.)
34-41	—Second Presentation—Inner/Passive/Relaxed (Soft presentation, no outer references or materials.)
41-48	—Third Presentation—Inner/Visual Imagery/Relaxed (Authoritative presentation, no outer references or materials.)
(41-48)	—(Practice session may alternate with or replace the third presentation.)
48-50	End of Class Sequence —Positive, encouraging suggestions.

---

3. Music Background
4. Relaxation
5. Positive Suggestions
6. Mind Calming
7. Teacher Credentials
8. Method Credibility
9. Visual Imagery
10. Bilateral Hemisphere Input
11. Multi-Sensory
12. Active Presentation
13. Non-Critical Correction
14. Whole-Brain Learning

References

Bancroft, W. J. The Psychology of Suggestopedia: Or Learning Without Stress. *Educational Courier*, February 1972, *42*(4), 16-19.

Bancroft, W. J. Foreign Language Teaching in Bulgaria. *Canadian Modern Language Review*, 1972, *28*(2), 9-13.

Bancroft, W. J. Education for the Future or the Lozanov System Revisited. *The Educational Courier*, 1973, *43*(8), 11-13.

Bancroft, W. J. The Lozanov Language Class. *The Journal of Suggestive-Accelerative Learning and Teaching*, Spring 1976, *1*(1), 48-74.

Bancroft, W. J. Suggestology and Suggestopedia: The Theory of the Lozanov Method. *The Journal of Suggestive-Accelerative Learning and Teaching*, Fall 1976, *1*(3), 187-216.

Brandwein, P., and R. Ornstein. The Duality of the Mind. *Instructor*, 1977, *86*, 54-59.

Buzan, T. *Use Both Sides of Your Brain*. New York: E. P. Dutton, 1976.

Caskey, O. L., and M. H. Flake. *Suggestive-Accelerative Learning: Adaptations of the Lozanov Method.* Des Moines: SALT, 1976.

Ferguson, M. *The Brain Revolution.* New York: Taplinger Publishing Company, 1973.

Galin, D. Educating Both Halves of the Brain. *Childhood Education*, October 1976, *53*, 17-20.

Hunter, M. Right-Brained Kids in Left-Brained Schools. *Today's Education*, November 1976, *65*, 45-48.

Lozanov, G. *Suggestologiya.* Sofia, Bulgaria: Izdatelsvo Nauka i Izkoustvo, 1971.

Lozanov, G. The Suggestological Theory of Communication and Instruction. *Suggestology and Suggestopedia*, 1975, *1*(3), 1-13.

Lozanov, G. Research Institute of Suggestology, First International Symposium of the Problems of Suggestology; Sofia, Bulgaria. English translation by Dr. Gabriel Racle. *Suggestopedia-Canada*, July 1977, 1-4.

Racle, G. A Suggestopedic Experiment in Canada. *Suggestology and Suggestopedia*, 1975, *1*(1), 45-51.

Racle, G. The Key Principles of Suggestopedia. *The Journal of Suggestive-Accelerative Learning and Teaching*, Fall 1976, *1*(3), 149-163.

Rennels, M. R. Cerebral Symmetry: An Urgent Concern for Education. *Phi Delta Kappan*, March 1976, *57*, 471-472.

Samples, R. E. Are You Teaching Only One Side of the Brain? *Learning*, February 1975, 25-28.

Samples, R. E. Mind Cycles and Learning. *Phi Delta Kappan*, May 1977, *58*, 688-692.

Schuster, D., R. Benitez-Bordon, and C. Gritton. *Suggestive-Accelerative Learning and Teaching: A Manual of Classroom Procedures Based on the Lozanov Method.* Des Moines: The Society for Suggestive-Accelerative Learning and Teaching, 1976.

Tart, C. T. *States of Consciousness*. New York: E. P. Dutton, 1975.

III.

DESIGN FORMAT AND OUTCOMES

It is not easy to find specific directions for carrying out suggestive-accelerative techniques in the classroom. Much of the literature deals more with the history, philosophy, and research than with what to do and how to do it. Practically none of Lozanov's early writing and little of his more recent efforts give details of teaching techniques or class activities. His talks at conferences contain more details but not of sufficient substance to direct application to classrooms. This is largely due to the essence of the method, which is complex and personal as well as attitudinal and situational. Such things do not readily lend themselves to specification, how-to-do-it manuals, or step-by-step application. Be that as it may, if the method is to have widespread use, it must be translated in ways that teachers can use in typical class settings. While it would be nice to attend a training session at the Institute or work for a time at one of the places where research projects or teaching programs are in progress, if suggestive-accelerative techniques are to be used and evaluated, such avenues are far too limited.

That the components can be identified and used is as real as the results which have been obtained in the experiments. There are hundreds of teachers in the United States who apply some or all of the suggestive-accelerative techniques on a more or less regular classroom basis (of course, almost all teachers use some of the components at one time or another as a part of effective teaching). Few of them have observed original Lozanov classes and even fewer have any specific training from the Institute or other educational agencies.

American applications of suggestive-accelerative learning have dealt with other subject areas more than with language. While the results have not matched the learning increments achieved in language, for reasons previously discussed, there is still reason to pursue even further applications of the methodology. Certainly, some techniques are more generally applicable than others, and some components easier to implement in selected learning settings. Methods appropriate for first grade spelling, fifth grade remedial reading, eighth grade earth science, high school literature, and university level courses of all types necessarily differ.

Teachers of foreign language at secondary and university levels obviously have the most extensive material and directions to assist them in using suggestive-accelerative teaching techniques. Many teachers have developed suggestive-accelerative procedures which have been effective by working with the basic Lozanov (1971, 1975) references, or even the secondary references available in English. The minimum essentials would probably include Bancroft (1972a, 1972b, 1973, 1976a, 1976b), Caskey and Flake (1976), Racle (1975, 1976), and Schuster *et al.* (1976). Teachers at all levels of other subject areas would also benefit from the greater detail of the philosophy and methodology contained in these references, since it is only summarized in this manual. Perusal of the articles in the *Journal of Suggestive-Accelerative Learning and Teaching*, inaugurated by the Society for Suggestive-Accelerative Learning and Teaching in 1976, would be similarly recommended for all levels and areas.

Limitations do not permit examples of activities, class sequences, and lesson plans for all subjects and levels; however, a sampling of these practical illustrations is included in the following section. With the fundamental concepts covered in earlier sections and the outline of the components which support the methodology, interested classroom teachers, hopefully, can develop a selection of elements and sequences which would be appropriate for the intended class and subject. Some modification will be necessary in every application. The essential ingredient and the one common to all would be an interest in trying some of the techniques, individually or collectively, with the same positive expectations necessary for the success of the class. Anything less works against an effective application.

Remedial Reading Class (Secondary Level and Above)

The Georgia Suggestopedia project has been developing methods of teaching remedial reading in the middle elementary grades since 1974. Both the tangible research results (mean gains of over 17 months on oral and silent reading with nine-month gains on word recognition after 16 weeks of 45-minute daily classes) and the intangible observations of those involved lead to the conclusion that SALT techniques work well as a reading methodology (Pritchard, 1974, and Pritchard and Taylor, 1976). Experience with adults and in college classes with individuals who evidence reading deficiencies indicate SALT approaches work equally well with the older student. A sequence and procedure which have been used in several recent such classes provide a more detailed illustration.

The 50-minute standard class alternates a SALT method of presenting material with individual reading lab work on a daily basis. Using the Programs for Achievement in Reading (PAR) which has materials for both power reading, *Reading for Power,* and speed reading, *Reading for Speed,* has been most effective (Smith, Brownsword, and Hanley, 1973). This series is built around short stories, work activities, word lists, and short standardized progress tests for each story. The high interest level for older students is helpful, as are the progress graphs for comprehension and speed checks, which are student initiated.

Alternating emphasis on power (comprehension) and speed of reading helps maintain interest, while the advanced content and positive experience with progress checks help sustain motivation. The class period dealing with content usually follows the standard SALT sequence, since the first few class meetings are devoted to explaining the approach and teaching relaxation techniques. The lab period is a traditional one using machines, taped programs, and self-paced experiences, although at times a music background is added.

Preparation—Physical Exercises. A brief period of physical exercises (two to three minutes) is used to lead into the relaxation and breathing components, which are important prerequisites to mind calming. If classes are taught progressive muscle relaxation (see Appendix for a sample script), these elements—exercise and relaxation—may be combined using the tense-and-relax sequence. In either case, the simple physical exercises have been found to be helpful with pre-school to adult level learners. Figure 4 provides examples in several exercises which can be used in a few minutes after classes become familiar with them.

Preparation—Relaxation Sequence. Regardless of the relaxation type taught or used by students (progressive muscle, psychological, or autogenic), a daily relaxation sequence of four or five minutes helps the class move into the relaxed state. Figure 5 is a typical script for such directions. If progressive muscle relaxation is preferred, a daily script of the same type will be found in the Appendix.

Preparation—Mind Calming. To insure further relaxation and receptive attitude, mind-calming exercises, which take only one or two minutes, are used as a lead-in to the presen-

Figure 4

Physical Exercises

While any of the less strenuous physical exercises which are appropriate for the age level and classroom conditions may be used, some which have been favorites of SALT teachers in recent years are briefly outlined below. For younger children, commercial exercise records have a number of suitable exercises with music background. Few records may be used in their entirety, since some exercises are not appropriate for classroom use but were developed for gym or playground groups. Several records with good exercises will be found listed in the "Resources" chapter.

Turtle Exercise (May be done sitting or standing)

Part 1   Tense left side of throat—hold—relax.
Tense right side of throat—hold—relax.
Tense center portion of throat—hold—relax.
Tense whole throat—hold. (Repeat three times.)

Part 2   Tense neck—relax neck—allow head to drop to chest.
Tense neck—pull head erect (vertically) under tension—hold.
Relax neck—allow head to drop to chest. (Repeat three times.)

Part 3   Tense neck—pull down as far as possible (try to touch ears with shoulders)—hold—relax.
Tense neck—stretch neck up as far as possible—hold—relax. (Repeat three times.)

Part 4   Tense neck—rotate head under tension to right three times—relax.
Tense neck—rotate head under tension to left three times—relax.
Drop head to chest—rotate three times to left and then three times to right without tension—head settles in relaxed position on chest. (Good exercise to continue with other activities at this point—either with eyes open or closed.)

(Continued on Next Page)

Figure 4 (Continued)

Diagonal Stretching (Standing) (Sometimes called the Apple Picking Exercise.)

Part 1   Stand with legs comfortably apart, arms at side.
          Stretch left hand as high as possible, pulling right leg off floor. (Repeat three times.)
Part 2   Stretch right hand as high as possible, pulling left leg off floor. (Repeat three times.)

Side Bends (Standing)

Part 1   Stand erect with legs together, arms at side.
          Move left hand down side of body without bending knees (right hand may be extended above head, if desired).
          When extended as far as possible, bounce to loosen muscles.
          Return to erect position—relax. (Repeat three times.)
Part 2   Move right hand down side of body in same manner as above.
          Return to erect position—relax. (Repeat three times.)

Toe Touching (Standing)

Any standard toe touching procedure may be used.

Deep Breathing (Standing or sitting)

Deep breathing exercises in unison, emphasizing holding.
Inhale—filling chest cavity—hold for count of 2—exhale—exhausting air completely (force air out). Relax on exhale. Repeat holding breath for longer counts (4—6—8) after practice.

Figure 5

Daily Class Relaxation Sequence: Physical and Mental Relaxation Types

---

Sit in your chair in any way that seems comfortable for you. Begin to relax and let your mind wander. Do not think of anything specific. Just settle back and begin to relax. Jiggle your legs up and down a few times and then let them drop loosely with your feet flat on the floor. Hold your arms down at your sides and shake them vigorously, then allow them to drop comfortably in your lap. You should be feeling even more relaxed now. Now swing your head around slowly several times in wide, loose circles, and let it settle forward in a comfortable, relaxed position. Let your eyes slowly close and take a deep breath. Exhale very slowly as you relax. Continue to relax as you concentrate on the sensation of floating. Floating down through your chair, downward-downward-downward. A good, heavy, relaxed feeling. Feel how relaxed and comfortable you are.

To increase the feeling of relaxation, I want you to think the word "relax" as you breathe out. Now, begin breathing deeply, regularly, slowly. Inhale slowly and deeply, taking in as much air as you can hold. Hold the air a moment, then slowly exhale. Do not breathe through your mouth. Inhale, hold, say to yourself, "relax," as you exhale. Feel your lungs fill with air as you slowly inhale. Experience the slow fall of your stomach as you exhale slowly, staying relaxed as you do so. Your whole body is now more and more relaxed. Your mind is calm, tranquil, and peaceful.

Keep breathing slowly and deeply, and concentrate on feeling relaxed as I talk to you about relaxing easily and quickly. Notice the warm sensation that flows over you as you relax. Enjoy it. Savor it. Notice how full relaxation feels. Feel the relaxation as you breathe deeply. Waves of relaxation travel from head to toe. Notice how comfortable you feel. If any parts of your body are tense, you might like to concentrate on relaxing them. (10-second pause) At times, it helps to visualize a quiet scene. Any scene that is pleasant and comfortable will do. It can be a lake with a sail boat, or a blue sky with fluffy clouds floating by, or a beautiful mountain, or a quiet stream, or a peaceful desert, or a green pasture. Anything that is quiet and pleasant and that you like. (10-second pause) It might be helpful for you to just let your mind be calm and tranquil as you tell yourself to relax physically and mentally. In your own way, relax as totally as you can. (10-second pause)

(Continued on Next Page)

Figure 5 (Continued)

In a relaxed state, you experience a feeling of well-being and optimism that allows you to absorb new ideas more easily, to retain them longer, and repeat them readily. You are more and more receptive to the new materials and ideas which will be presented to you. You can think more clearly and concentrate more easily. You have a greater feeling of personal well-being. You are relaxed but alert. Calm but attentive. If you have any difficulty recalling any of the material covered today, simply take a breath—exhale slowly—and say to yourself, "relax." You will find what you were trying to remember will return much more readily.

Now I am going to count from one to three. At the count of three, let your eyes open but retain your relaxed, tranquil feeling. Maintain your state of alertness and awareness, while your teacher presents new and interesting material to you. Ready. 1–2–3. Let your eyes open, everyone. Now listen with attention and interest to the new material. (Approximate time—4-1/2 minutes. Continue with presentation of new material.)

- - - - - - - - - - - - - - (Presentation of New Material) - - - - - - - - - - - - - - -

(End of class.) All right. Now everyone let your eyes close once more. Take a deep breath. Exhale slowly. Relax and allow what you have learned to sink inward. Slowly, deeply, indelibly. Recall the interesting and informative material which has been covered today.

Now I am going to count from one to five. At the count of five, let your eyes open and return to your normal state of awareness; refreshed, alert, feeling good. You will feel wide awake and energetic. You will feel stronger and more capable. You will find it easier to be cheerful and optimistic. Your work and your day will go better and easier.

tation of the new material. Figure 6 is a typical exercise of this type.

Preparation—Visual Imagery. Visual imagery may be used at this stage, if it is helpful in either furthering the relaxed, positive, and receptive state of the learner or as a specific prelude to new material which may be covered (see English Literature example which follows). Visual imagery exercises may be of the general type, such as "The Mountain Valley," found in the Appendix, or any general descriptive scene which promotes imagery. It may also be combined with either Early Pleasant Recollection Exercises, such as in Figure 7, or of the Early Pleasant Learning Restimulation type (Figure 12), both of which are designed to prepare the learner both physically and mentally for learning new material. Some teachers prefer to use visual imagery exercises in the active part of the material presentation or in the practice session following the presentation. While these exercises are helpful and might be used in several places, time limitations usually permit only one visual imagery exercise during a typical class period unless they are an integral part of the material content.

Presentation of New Material—First Presentation. The first presentation of the new material is the reading of the short story to the class by the instructor in a normal straightforward tone of voice while the class follows the story in their texts. If, for some reason, the music background has not been used in the daily class activities to this point, it is important that it be provided during the presentation of new material.

Presentation of New Material—Second Presentation. The second presentation involves the reading of the story to the class in a soft, barely audible, voice while the class relaxes with eyes closed.

Presentation of New Material—Third Presentation. The third, and final, reading of the story is in a commanding,

Figure 6

Mind-Calming Exercise—Little White Cloud
(All Levels)

Sit as comfortably as you can. Breathe easily and normally. Close your eyes and begin to relax.

Imagine that you are in the middle of a beautiful meadow. You are lying on your back on the grass on a warm, summer day. Above you there is a cloudless, blue sky. You are lying there relaxed, comfortable, and at ease with yourself. Far away on the horizon there appears a small, white cloud floating across the blue sky. The cloud moves slowly toward you, drifting gently across the sky.

You are relaxed, very much at peace with yourself, as you watch the cloud drift toward you. Finally, the white cloud stops directly overhead. You watch the white cloud as the calm, peaceful feeling spreads over you. Now you imagine projecting yourself into the cloud. You *are* the little white cloud, soaring over the meadow, calm and relaxed. See yourself as the little white cloud, peaceful and at ease with yourself, looking down on the beautiful green meadow. Drift gently over the meadow.

Now open your eyes and return to those around you while you remain completely calm and pleasantly relaxed.

Alternative 1: May also be used as a lead-in to a Fantasy Trip Exercise, as in the example which follows, or as an introduction to new material which will involve mental imagery.

Alternative 2: Follow-up discussions of feelings and visual images may be used with classes, particularly during the early use of the exercise.

Note: When used with lower grade levels, a simpler wording might be adopted.

Figure 7

Early Pleasant Recollection Exercise

Get as comfortable as you can. Take several deep breaths and begin to relax. Breathe in and out naturally. Close your eyes and let your mind go to any times when you were very, very happy. I want you to remember the times when you were happy. Remember as many happy times as you can.

Your happy times have been on special days, like birthdays, or Christmas, or visiting with family or friends. They might have been on a vacation or a trip somewhere. It might have been a time when you were very proud of something you had done. It might have been a time when you learned something, like riding a bicycle, fishing, or playing ball or a musical instrument.

Now, from the happy times you have remembered, select one to focus on. Choose one that you care to focus on and try to remember as much as you can about it. Try to recreate the time when you were very happy. Think about the happy time and all you can remember about it.

Were you alone or with others? Were you inside or outside? If you were inside, can you remember how the room or other place looked? If you were outside, what was the weather like? What were you wearing? What were the colors around you? Try to remember how you felt. Were there any special sounds or smells on your special, happy day? Take a few minutes and try to remember all you can about the time you were very happy. Now, return to those around you and retain your happy, contented feeling as we work together in class.

Discussion Questions (Used for a few times when exercise is first introduced)

Did the time go fast or slow as you thought about your special happy time?

Did you notice anything (or remember anything) that you have not noticed before when you thought about that time?

Did you remember how you felt? Happy feelings? Body feelings? What is the feeling of happy?

Can you still feel some of those happy feelings now?

---

authoritative, and dramatic manner while students provide as clear mental images of the story, its characters, and events, as possible. In some classes, due to time limitations, the visual imagery is emphasized in the second presentation and the third presentation is replaced by a practice session or a directed visual imagery experience related to the story content. Exercises, such as the Creative Writing Exercise in the Appendix, can be useful here.

Practice Session and Control Check. Students now read the story one or more times on their own, after which they work individually on the practice activity in the workbook accompanying the text. The activities are designed to focus the student on the content, word use, interpretation, and understanding. Finally, students take the self-administered test over the day's story and record their progress on the chart. From time to time, the teacher will ask for test scores to be turned in, or the class may agree in advance that one will be used for a daily grade.

Ending Session. Those who complete the class work early may relax and visualize the story for the day, read in another series text, or engage in any quiet free-choice activity until all are finished. A few minutes before the class is over, the teacher gains their attention, has them put reading materials away, and closes the class on a positive, suggestive note, as found at the end of the script in Figure 5.

English Literature Class Example (Sixth Grade and Above)

Many of the same SALT approaches found to be successful in remedial reading classes work equally well with regular literature classes. A sequence used in Wisconsin projects based on work by Held (1976) provides a typical example. The objectives for the SALT class sequence would be to: (1) stimulate imagery, (2) provide a meaningful language experience, (3) develop oral language, (4) provide a relaxed learning environment, and (5) provide word recognition skills.

Preparation Phase. The preparation phase begins with a brief physical exercise, such as those shown in Figure 4, followed by a mind-calming exercise, and ending with deep breathing exercises. Finally, a visual imagery exercise is used to introduce the lesson content and the daily activity. For the story, "The Sinking of the Edmund Fitzgerald," which has been read in class, a continuation activity might use the Fantasy Trip Exercise activity (Figure 8) to combine visual imagery and lead in to the day's task. The teacher directs the class (now engaged in the Fantasy Trip) to: "See yourself traveling over Lake Superior. Look down and imagine yourself seeing the sinking of the Edmund Fitzgerald. Imagine it as vividly as you can. See the water with the waves breaking over the bow of the ship. Look at all the details in your imagination. Sense the weather. See the sky and the water and the ship. You and only you see the ship sink." (Provide time for students to develop mental images.)

Active Phase. Use the Fantasy Trip exercise to move into the activity of the day: "Now that you have seen the sinking of the Edmund Fitzgerald, remember how it happened. Return to the here and now. Open your eyes and return to those around you. I want you to write about what you saw happen in the sinking. Write about what *really* happened as you visualize it. Only you know, so now share it by writing about it."

The class procedure is for students to develop a list of words used in stories which they are not sure how to spell. As the students write their stories, they add words to the list on their desks. The teacher moves around the room helping students and checking the word lists. The teacher also selects words from the students' lists and makes a simple flash-card on a 5 x 7 index card with a heavy black marker. When the

Figure 8

Fantasy Trip Exercise
(Balloon, Magic Carpet, Flying Saucer, Hang-Glider,
Bird, Cloud)

Objectives
>To calm mind and relax.
>To provide visual imagery experience.
>To develop sense of freedom.
>To provide context for concept development.
>To provide context for language experience.
>To provide basis for lesson.

Directions
>Sit comfortably in your chair and relax. Breathe normally. Close your eyes and attend to your breathing—in and out—easily, comfortably—rhythmically. This is an exercise to help you use your imagination and also make learning things in today's lesson much easier.

>Relax and imagine that you are lying on your back looking at a bright blue summer sky. It is a quiet and lazy day with a soft breeze blowing. You feel warm inside, at ease, and contented. As you watch the sky, you see (a small white, fluffy cloud) (a beautiful, multi-colored balloon) (a graceful bird) (a brightly colored soaring hang-glider) (an Arabian Nights Magic Carpet).

>It moves lazily and gently across the sky as you watch. In your imagination you (become the cloud) (are in the basket swinging under the balloon) (become the bird) (are soaring on the hang-glider) (are riding the magic carpet). You are high above the ground looking down on the scene below. The wind gently drifts you along as you watch the ground far below. (Continue with information to set stage for the day's new material or other activity.)

---

students have completed their stories, some are shared with the class. The class may be asked to relax and imagine the "sinking" as the student reads his or her story. When several stories are read, the teacher reads the word list which has been selected from the students' lists.

The teacher has students relax and concentrate on the word list. Each word is shown, using the prepared flash-cards while the students visualize the word, its meaning, and what it makes them think of. As students visualize the word, the teacher pronounces the word, spells it, and gives a brief definition or meaning. All words are reviewed in this manner.

Passive Phase. Students continue to relax with eyes closed listening to the music background. The instructor repeats each word on the list three times, using the normal, soft, and authoritative intonations, while the students mentally visualize the word. Words are repeated in a rhythmic manner as students relax and concentrate on the visual image of each word.

Control Check. The teacher presents the words on the list as a spelling check while students spell them. The check may or may not be taken up or recorded.

Art Class Example (Junior High and Above)

A class example using SALT techniques for student production rather than material coverage is illustrated by a class sequence typical of that found in the Iowa projects. Students have been gradually introduced to selected physical exercises, relaxation techniques, and visual imagery from the beginning of the semester. Each day some or all of these elements are used by the teacher. A music background is continually used throughout the class, either as a relaxing background or as a part of a specific class activity.

Preparation Phase. Students arriving in class are accustomed to going to their art tables and preparing for a few minutes of physical exercise. These usually include hand push exercises, stretching and leaning, and ending with head and neck relaxation. A mind-calming exercise is used following the physical activity, often with a direct lead-in to the visual imagery activity. The visual imagery exercise is typically selected to introduce the topic for the day. The visual imagery exercise selected will lead to the drawing activity for the day. For example, if contour drawing is to be the topic, the imagery would be directed to helping see how contours are "seen" by the eye. A brief outline of the exercise might be: "It is night. You are standing outside in the dark. You are alone and it is peaceful and relaxed. It is a perfect evening. The stars are out but there is no moon. You look around you and see outlines of things. You notice there are houses, trees, fences, buildings. In the dark, you see only the outlines and merely a hint of what they really are. Some you recognize easily. Many seem strange to you. See yourself standing in the dark, looking at the shapes all around you. It is a calm, peaceful feeling. Keep that peaceful, relaxed feeling as we begin our work for today. Today's lesson is on outline or contour drawing. Open your eyes and return to those around you in class, and we will get ready for what we are going to do today."

Presentation Phase—Active Session. The teacher continues with directions for the day's activity. "Get comfortable at your desks (on your stools) and relax. Look at the chair in the center of the room. On the chair you see an object (plant, bottle, etc.). Squint your eyes to take out the detail. This makes it look like it might at night—in outline form. Forget three-dimensional drawing. Look for an outline edge. Place your pencil on the paper and let your eye slowly follow the outline and your pencil follow as you watch the outline—slowly, slowly. See and feel the line. It is not important what your picture looks like—we are getting the feel for outline drawing. You are touching the line of the chair with your eyes and your pencil is an extension of that line through your eyes. (Teacher now moves around room as students draw.) Draw the chair and the object in contour form, trying to watch the chair and feel the line—not looking at your paper or your drawing." (Alternative activity would be to have students keep eyes closed to obtain a mental image of the subject of the drawing. Opening eyes occasionally to check visual references, students draw with eyes closed. If time permits, both variations may be used.)

Have students share drawings, emphasizing that all are different—but that all represent how they were seen by the person. Art is not right or wrong. Ask students to share difficulties in visualizing the subject for the drawing or difficulty in drawing with eyes closed (if that activity was used).

To end the class, a fun exercise is often used. "Position a clean sheet of paper on your board. Now just relax and listen to the music. Put your pencil in the center of the page and keep your eyes closed. Listen to the music and let the pencil move, following the music or beat. Let your hand flow to the music. Do not look at your paper. Continue until the music stops." At the end of the short (one-minute) music presentation, students may be asked to share papers. Discuss how they feel during the activity. Repeat the exercise using different types of music (slow, fast, loud, soft).

For this example, no passive phase, as such, would be identified. Some topics in art education, however, make extensive use of the passive phase, particularly through visual imagery. Art teachers using SALT methods teach art history and biographies of artists through this approach. Some teachers combine the techniques to get students to visualize *themselves* as great artists and draw or paint as if they were the artist in their mental imagery. Drawing from word descriptions can also use the extended visual imagery activity to move the class into a directed experience, but one which provides freedom from structure (see The Living Painting, Visual Imagery Memory, and Creative Writing exercises in the Appendix).

SALT Techniques in Early Childhood and Elementary Education

The use of SALT methodology in school settings with regularly scheduled class times for academic areas is a relatively easy adaptation. The appropriate applications of the techniques with lower grade levels require a somewhat different approach. Despite the advantage of longer periods of time during which to present material, young children's short attention span largely offsets the opportunity to work with them in the extended time frame. The use of SALT techniques can be adapted for early childhood and lower elementary levels, if one is careful to match the elements of the methodology to the developmental level of the students. Typically, this is achieved through either (1) abbreviation of the SALT methodology through shortening the sequence of elements to present a topic, exercise, or material in a 10- to 30-minute experience, or (2) presenting and practicing material through selection of one or two elements (i.e., music background and visual imagery) appropriate for the age level and material.

While Lozanov has written of his work with the elementary grades, and recently described a program which was essentially a K-12 project in the Bulgarian schools, little information on how he adapts his techniques for young children has been available. References to having a specially written opera prepared and used over national television to teach basic mathematics concepts in the early grades imply a more extensive program than is likely to occur in this country in the near future.

There is increasing evidence that suggestive-accelerative techniques lend themselves quite well to early concept learning. At least four basic principles may be identified for which Suggestopedic applications have been found to be most appropriate.

The first is the obvious theorem that simple concepts are easier to understand and comprehend than complex ones.

A second basic principle is the fact that prior relevant information has a significant effect in conceptual learning. The theory of transfer, by whatever definition one chooses, is of the essence here. One of the most fundamental conclusions in learning is that transfer is enhanced by methods which are designed to facilitate transfer. Put in another way, one must teach for transfer if transfer is to occur. Suggestive-accelerative methods include techniques which are specifically designed to utilize previously learned information and build upon them in sound ways to insure higher levels of conceptual learning on the part of the child.

A third principle may be stated in a negative way for emphasis. There is ample evidence that low level attending skills, higher levels of anxiety and tension, and lower self-concepts negatively affect concept formation. Early concept learning may be effective only to the point that such interferences and distractions do not diminish the learning which occurs. Again, the techniques which are involved in suggestive-accelerative learning approaches are designed to increase attention, reduce tension, and heighten self-concepts on the part of the child.

A fourth major principle involved in early concept formation is that visual imagery increases the learning of concepts. For the young child, this becomes particularly important, and may well be *the* most essential factor in a number of kinds of readiness. Language acquisition and later attainment of reading skills depend in large measure upon the child's developing ever increasing capacities for visual imagery as it relates to both concrete visual acuity and constructive perception. Suggestive-accelerative techniques emphasize visual imagery as an essential part of the Suggestopedic process.

Spelling Class Example—Primary Grades

The adaptation of SALT methodology to the lower grades may occasionally follow the general outline of similar applications at higher grade levels, with the exception of the type of activities used in the process. An example would be the following SALT sequence for a spelling activity at the primary grade level.

Preparation. Physical exercises, such as outlined in Figure 4 or those available on commercial records, work well with young children. Occasionally, a selection of exercises is used by the teacher to tie in to the content of the lesson (i.e., spelling parts of the body or body actions). It is most helpful if children learn by experience that the physical exercise activity ends with them either sitting or lying on the floor (or mats) and with a quiet, relaxing exercise. This is particularly helpful as a prelude to other relaxation or visual imagery exercises.

It has been found that young children need breathing exercises, preferably at the end of the physical exercise section, and they respond well to positive suggestion regarding the relaxed state of body parts. This is a better activity than the tense-relax sequence, at least up through the middle elementary grades ("Do your arms feel relaxed? Shake them and make them feel loose and relaxed. See how good they feel. Nice and loose and relaxed. Let them feel good and relaxed.").

An important element with young children is to provide specific activities in sense focusing and sense awareness. Activities such as those in Figures 9, 10, and 11 work well. They

Figure 9

Sense Focusing:
Sounds Around Us—Listening Awareness Exercise
(All Levels)

Although we listen all the time, sometimes we do not hear many of the sounds around us. We hear more things when we are relaxed and we hear more things when our eyes are closed to avoid the distractions of things we see. Now, sit comfortably, close your eyes, breathe normally, and begin to relax. Everyone is going to be as quiet at they can be, and we are going to listen to all the sounds we can for a few minutes. Try to identify all the things you can hear. Now, listen carefully to everything you can for a minute or two. Keep your eyes closed and listen. Later we will see how many sounds you can remember. (Allow two to three minutes to listen.)

Now, open your eyes.

Discussion Questions

What things did you hear? (Identify sounds heard in the room, outside the room, inner body sounds—heart beats, breathing, any others.)

Did you have a mental picture of what made the sounds? What were some of them?

What kind of picture did you have when you couldn't identify the sound?

Did the time seem like a very long time as you listened? How long do you think it was?

Have you ever tried this sort of thing? At the seashore, on a lake, in a forest, in your room?

Listening skills, like other skills, improve with practice. We will do this exercise several times during the next week or so, and you will find that you will be able to listen more sharply with practice. You might try it on your own to see what sort of sounds are around your house or neighborhood.

Figure 10

Sense Focusing:
Body Feelings—Touch Awareness Exercise

Our sense of touch enables us to contact and interpret our surroundings. We depend on it, but may not think about how we use it. Sit as comfortably as you can, close your eyes, breathe naturally, and relax. Focus on your sense of touch as I call your attention to feelings.

Focus your attention to your head—is anything touching it? Do you feel your hair? Glasses? A hair ribbon? Think of your body feelings. Where do your clothes touch you? Around your neck? Waist? Knees? Ankles? Do they feel loose, comfortable, or tight? Is there any place that is a stronger or heavier touch than others, such as a belt or sash, or cuffs on a shirt or sweater? Feel your socks and shoes. Do they feel loose, comfortable, or tight? Do you have on rings, bracelets, necklaces? Focus your attention on them. Are your legs crossed? Do you feel the pressure when they touch? If so, uncross them and see the difference. Are your hands in your lap? Do you feel their pressure on your legs? Concentrate on the feeling of where parts of your body touch each other. Focus your feelings where you are touching your chair. Feel the pressure?

Now, sort of "sweep" your attention from your head to your feet, thinking about how your sense of touch provides information about your feelings to you. Sweep down from head to feet and then back up to your head, thinking about the feelings of touch.

Now, open your eyes, and return to the people around you.

Discussion Questions
Was it difficult to focus your attention on your body feelings? Were you aware that some of your clothing or jewelry was tight? Loose? Comfortable?

If anything was uncomfortable, why were you not aware of it?

Figure 11

Sense Focusing:
Inside Body Feelings—Awareness Exercise

Today we are going to focus our awareness to feelings inside our bodies. Sit as comfortably as you can, breathe naturally, close your eyes, and start to relax. I am going to call your attention to parts of your body while you focus your thoughts on them.

Think of your left hand. Focus all your thoughts on your left hand. Send all your thoughts down your arm to your left hand. Feel it as much as you can. Now, send your thoughts to your right hand. Focus on your right hand. Feel your right hand. Now, bring your thoughts deep inside your chest. Now, think of your stomach. Focus your awareness on your stomach. Now, send your thoughts down to your right foot. Send all your thoughts there. Feel your right foot. Now, think about your skin. Focus on your skin. Now, send your thoughts inside your bones. Think about your bones, deep inside your body. Feel them. Now, bring your thoughts back into your head. Let your mind go where it will.

Now, open your eyes and gently return to the people around you.

Discussion Questions

When do you usually think about the inside of your body?

What usually calls your attention to the inside of your body?

Can people really "feel things in their bones"?

Did you have difficulty centering your thoughts on any part of the body we talked about?

---

may be used as written, beginning with the third or fourth grade, although a simpler explanation should be used for the primary grades. After repeating the exercises a number of times, children need little in the way of specific focusing direction and enjoy the exercises, sometimes on a daily basis. Sense focusing leads naturally to mind calming and beginning visual imagery exercises. It has been found that the mind-calming and environmental walk exercises may be used almost verbatim after the third grade, and simpler versions work quite well below that level. Environmental walks emphasizing visual imagery in the primary grades should start with familiar places, such as walking to school, playing in a neighborhood park, shopping in a nearby supermarket or department store, or asking them to visualize their own houses or rooms. Specific visual imagery experiences should also use the exercises designed to learn imagery, such as found in the Appendix. At times, the Early Pleasant Learning Restimulation Exercise (Figure 12) is most helpful in setting a positive, suggestive atmosphere for learning. The same can be said for the Early Pleasant Recollection Exercise described earlier (Figure 7).

Presentation of New Material. The teacher presents the new spelling words (from five to 20 words, depending on grade level and lesson objectives) as children relax with eyes closed lying on the floor or mats. The words are covered three times using the normal, soft, and authoritative intonations. Each word is pronounced, spelled, and pronounced again in a rhythmic cadence, with dramatic inflections when appropriate to the word, particularly during the third presentation. Children try to visualize each word as it is repeated; first the word as it appears in print, then the letters as the word is spelled, and then what the word reminds them of during the final pronunciation. Some teachers prefer to apply a mental image related to the presentation with a visual image

Figure 12

*Early Pleasant Learning Restimulation Exercise
(Elementary Level and Above)*

Students are relaxed with eyes closed with a music background.

Sit comfortably with your eyes closed and just relax as much as you can. Feel nice and relaxed while you let your mind wander wherever it will. When our thoughts take us to other places, frequently they take us to happy times in the past. Our thoughts go to when we were happy or having a good time. Many of our happy thoughts and memories of good times are of times when we learned something.

Think of the times when you learned something and it was a happy, fun time. There have been many such times in the past, so just try to remember several of them. It might have been when you were very young and learning some things for the first time, like how to ride a tricycle or bicycle—or catch a ball—or tie your shoes—or print your name. It might be something specific like learning to sing a song or a general feeling of learning like learning to read. It might be something that happened more recently like learning to fish—or play a musical instrument —or cook a favorite food—or an interesting hobby. It might be an active thing, like sports or athletics, or a quiet pastime or something in school. Think of many times when you have been happy learning something.

Now, from all the pleasant learning experiences you have thought of, pick one to think about more in detail. Pick one of your happy learning memories. Everyone have one? Fine! Now picture your pleasant learning experience in your mind as I ask you some questions to help you remember as much as you can about it.

Where were you when you learned the things you are remembering? Were you alone or were there others with you? If others were with you, who were they? Where were you—at home, at school, on a playground? Were you inside or outside? If you were outside, what was the weather like? If you were inside, can you visualize the room or location? Remember as much about the time as you can.

Now, I want you to think about how you felt when you were learning. See yourself learning. How did you feel? What thoughts were you thinking? How did your body feel during this happy learning time? Recall how you were thinking and feeling. See how interested and

(Continued on Next Page)

Figure 12 (Continued)

eager to learn you were. See how you felt about learning something new. See how pleasant it feels to learn.

Now hang on to those pleasant feelings about learning. Keep those feelings as we learn some new things today. Open your eyes and return to those around you while you keep the pleasant, happy, comfortable feeling of learning new and interesting things.

Note: Directions and specific examples may be changed somewhat to be more appropriate for the lower grade levels or adult learners.

Figure 13

Early Concept Learning Activity

Subject:	Parts of the Body Identification.
Grade Level:	Pre-School/Kindergarten/First Grade.
Prerequisites:	Previous passive listening exercises (ability to listen and follow directions).

Behavioral
Objectives:

1. Listen actively with music background.
2. Responding to verbal directions.
3. As a result of Activity I, the child will identify parts of the body after listening to verbal cues.
4. As a result of Activity II, the child will identify parts of the body while carrying out a directed action.

Materials
Needed:

1. Background music.
2. List of body parts.
3. Flannel board doll (optional).

Presentation:

I. First Activity
1. Children are sitting in a circle, relaxed to music background.
2. Review all parts of the body which will be identified in the exercise by demonstrating with one of the children (flannel board doll or any large doll may be used).
3. Direct children to listen very carefully and carry out the activity (follow directions).
4. As children listen to directions, the teacher identifies body parts, one at a time and the children point to the appropriate body part on their own bodies.
5. Examples:
   a. Point to your nose.
   b. Point to an ear.
   c. Point to an eye.
   d. (Continue with other body parts.)

II. Second Activity
1. Children are standing, music background.

(Continued on Next Page)

Figure 13 (Continued)

2. The teacher identifies a body part and gives a directed action at the same time, after which the children carry out the appropriate action.
3. Examples:
   a. Touch your left ear.
   b. Wave your right hand.
   c. Blink your eyes.
   d. Point to your elbow.
   e. Scratch your head.
   f. Stand on your right foot.
   g. Touch your right foot with your left hand.
   h. (Continue with other activities.)
4. A delayed response may be used by giving children time to think about action and then responding together on signal from the teacher.

Control of Error:

1. Children observing each other for additional cues where needed.
2. Teacher adding action on his or her part to guide children who do not respond correctly.

Competency Evaluation:

1. Begin with simple directions and body parts which can be easily identified by the group, then proceed to more difficult responses.
2. All children should respond correctly to the pointing exercise before moving to the other exercises.
3. Most children should respond to the activities correctly, but some children will have difficulty with the more complex directions until they are familiar with the process.

Variations:

1. If children experience difficulty with more complex directions, discussion or sharing (some children helping other children) may be used until body parts are known and actions are correctly carried out.
2. For older groups, a "Simon Says" format may be used in a non-competitive way (i.e., no elimina-

(Continued on Next Page)

Figure 13 (Continued)

tion from the activity for an incorrect response since this is a learning activity, not a game).

3. If possible, videotape the exercise and let children see themselves responding to the directions, using a segment when children are responding correctly.

4. Activities may be carried out with children sitting at their desks, if the actions are carefully selected.

Home Application:

1. Parents can either use the exercises as an individual game with children or incorporate the actions and directions in everyday relationships with children.

2. When reading or looking at pictures in books or magazines, ask child to identify body parts (or have child identify body part and then ask child to point to similar part ("Point to *your* toe.").

3. Have child carry out actions found in stories involving body parts ("Hop on both feet like a bunny.").

of each whole word on the first (normal) presentation, an image of what it means or reminds one of during the second (soft) presentation, and an emphasis on the letters as the words are spelled during the third (authoritative) presentation. As an alternative, the teacher may have students follow the spelling of the words while looking at word lists or spelling texts during either the first or third presentation (but not both presentations).

Practice—Passive Session. The children now relax on the floor with eyes closed while the teacher pronounces the words and spells the words in cadence to music. The list may be repeated in the same manner in a soft voice, if time permits.

Practice—Dramatic Session. The children assemble in groups of four or five and the teacher gives each group a word or group of words from the list. The group decides how to act out or demonstrate the words they have been given (charade type). Each group presents a word in turn while the other groups watch and try to guess the word. For older children, or as an alternate activity, the children in the other groups write down the words that are dramatized and the lists are turned in (or self-graded) for a later control check.

Ending Session. The children have a short time at the end of the period to relax to music without specific directions or suggested activities.

Concept Development Example—Early Childhood Level

The use of SALT techniques in early concept and language acquisition is more of an adaptation of short, often repeated exercises than an extended period of activity in typical school settings. The teacher may select from any of the basic concepts which are a part of pre-school, kindergarten, or first grade objectives, such as parts of the body, colors, positional or relational concepts, or other areas, and develop exercises

Figure 14

SALT Instructional and Individual Goals

SALT Element	Instructional Purpose	Student Objective
1. Comfortable Classroom	Encourages students. Identifies class as pleasant setting and a place for learning. Prepares student to attend and learn. Feelings more important than decor. Aids student's feeling of importance as a person.	Classrooms are "nice" places, "good" things happen here. I feel "good" here. I belong here. I like this class.
2. General Positive Suggestions	Promotes relaxed, encouraging atmosphere. Increases receptivity of class and individuals. Adds to credibility of method and teacher. Aids sense of purpose and feelings of belonging.	Learning can be fun. Students can learn. The class can learn easily. We are going to accomplish a lot.
3. Relaxation Exercises	Prepares for mind calming. Clears mind for learning. Reduces anxiety and tension. Produces general feeling of well-being. Increases receptivity.	This is a pleasant experience. I am beginning to feel better. I can think and concentrate better.
4. Mind-Calming Exercises	Mental (psychological) relaxation. Prepares students for new material. Establishes receptivity. Clears	My mind is becoming clear. I have put aside distractions and interferences. I can concentrate

(Continued on Next Page)

Figure 14 (Continued)

SALT Element	Instructional Purpose	Student Objective
	anxieties and distraction. Provides imagery experiences.	more easily on the lesson.
5. Specific Suggestions	Personalized suggestions. Aids self-concept, promotes learning through encouragement. Fosters receptivity. Establishes belief that learning will occur.	I can learn. I can do the work, solve the problems, understand the exercises. Learning is fun and easy. I believe in myself.
6. Music Background	Acts as carrier for material into right hemisphere. Aids in furthering relaxed state, both physically and mentally. Has cultural and aesthetic properties for class and individuals.	This is helpful, soothing, and relaxing. This helps me focus my attention on the lesson. The music is pretty and makes me feel good.
7. Rhythmic, Varied Intonation	Repetition of material is reinforcing. Increases attention and interest. Emphasizes importance of material. Adds to short- and long-term memory by enhancing retention.	This is different and interesting. This must be important. This helps me learn and remember.
8. Active and Passive Presentations	Provides variety of material presentation. Contrast aids interest and attention span. Relaxed state fosters creativity and permits generalizations and applications.	I understand what is going on. I understand the material. I find it easy to pay attention. I can learn and remember.

based on SALT elements. The activity outline found in the Appendix works quite well here. An example of the teaching of body parts utilizing such an approach is found in Figure 13. Experience has shown that these types of exercises can be developed for 10- to 20-minute experiences and can be repeated, often adding more complex elements throughout the school year. It is best to use groups of children numbering eight to ten, although some activities are successful with class-sized groups. The learning center concept, where the class rotates between assigned areas of the class or to specific activities, is very useful in that one activity can be a SALT experience, thus involving fewer students in the group.

The use of SALT techniques in teaching concepts at the elementary level or in adapting typical lesson plan activities can be a relatively easy step for an interested teacher. The instructional purposes for all grade levels in a general way parallel the instructional purposes related to each SALT element. The relationship of the SALT elements, instructional purposes, and student objectives are outlined in Figure 14. It is obvious that these are not related exclusively to the elementary grades, although they may be more easily adapted in activities common to the lower grade levels. The interested teacher, however, will find that there are numerous opportunities to integrate SALT elements without either a major change in the instructional or behavioral objectives or deviation from the classroom atmosphere which is believed to be appropriate for the respective grade level.

References

Bancroft, W. J. The Psychology of Suggestopedia: Or Learning Without Stress. *Educational Courier*, February 1972a, *42*(4), 16-19.

Bancroft, W. J. Foreign Language Teaching in Bulgaria. *Canadian Modern Language Review*, 1972b, *28*(2), 9-13.

Bancroft, W. J. Education for the Future or the Lozanov System Revisited. *The Educational Courier*, 1973, *43*(8), 11-13.

Bancroft, W. J. The Lozanov Language Class. *The Journal of Suggestive-Accelerative Learning and Teaching*, Spring 1976a, *1*, 48-74.

Bancroft, W. J. Suggestology and Suggestopedia: The Theory of the Lozanov Method. *The Journal of Suggestive-Accelerative Learning and Teaching*, Fall 1976b, *1*(3), 187-216.

Caskey, O. L., and M. H. Flake. *Essentials of Suggestopedia: A Primer for Practitioners*, ERIC, 1976.

Caskey, O. L., and M. H. Flake. *Suggestive-Accelerative Learning: Adaptations of the Lozanov Method*. Des Moines: SALT, 1976.

Held, D. *The Effect of the Lozanov Method for Teaching Word Meaning to Fifth and Sixth Graders*. Unpublished doctoral dissertation, Iowa State University, 1976.

Held, D. Suggestive-Accelerative Learning and Teaching: An Experiment with the Elements of an Altered States Approach in Reading. *Journal of Suggestive-Accelerative Learning and Teaching*, Summer 1976, *1*(2), 131-136.

Lozanov, G. *Suggestologiya*. Sofia, Bulgaria: Izdatelsvo Nauka i Izkoustvo, 1971.

Lozanov, G. *Problems of Suggestology*. New York: Gordon and Breach Science Publishers, Inc., 1975.

Lozanov, G. Suggestopedia in Primary Schools. *Suggestology and Suggestopedia*, 1975, *1*(2), 1-14.

Lozanov, G. The Suggestological Theory of Communication and Instruction. *Suggestology and Suggestopedia*, 1975, *1*(3), 1-13.

Prichard, A. *An Altered States Approach to Remedial Read-*

ing Instruction. Atlanta: Georgia State Department of Education, 1974.

Prichard, A., and J. Taylor. Adapting the Lozanov Method for Remedial Reading Instruction. *Journal of Suggestive-Accelerative Learning and Teaching,* Summer 1976, *1*(2), 107-115.

Prichard, A., and J. Taylor. An Altered States Approach to Remedial Reading Instruction. *The Educational Courier,* 1976, *46*(2).

Racle, G. A Suggestopedic Experiment in Canada. *Suggestology and Suggestopedia,* 1975, *1*(1), 45-51.

Racle, G. The Key Principles of Suggestopedia. *The Journal of Suggestive-Accelerative Learning and Teaching,* Fall 1976, *1*(3), 149-163.

Schuster, D., R. Benitez-Bordon, and C. Gritton. *Suggestive-Accelerative Learning and Teaching: A Manual of Classroom Procedures Based on the Lozanov Method.* Des Moines: SALT, 1976.

Smith, B.M., W. Brownsword, and G. Hanley. *Reading for Power.* Providence, Rhode Island: P.A.R., Inc., 1973.

Smith, B.M., W. Brownsword, and G. Hanley. *Reading for Speed.* Providence, Rhode Island: P.A.R., Inc., 1973.

IV.

RESOURCES

Suggestive-Accelerative Learning

The Society for Suggestive-Accelerative Learning and Teaching, Inc.
2740 Richmond Avenue
Des Moines, Iowa 50317
(Charles Gritton, Membership Chairman and Business Manager)

The Journal for Suggestive-Accelerative Learning and Teaching
Dr. Donald Schuster, Editor
Department of Psychology
Iowa State University
Ames, Iowa 50011

SALT Newsletter
Dr. Owen Caskey, Editor
College of Education
P. O. Box 4560
Texas Tech University
Lubbock, Texas 79409

Bancroft, W. J. Civilization and Diversity: Foreign Language Teaching in Bulgaria. *Canadian Modern Language Review*, 1973, *29*(25), 8-14.

Biggers, J. L., and M. E. Stricherz. Relaxation and Suggestion in a Recognition Task. *Journal of Suggestive-Accelerative Learning and Teaching*, Summer 1976, *1*(2), 100-106.

Caskey, O. L. Suggestopedic Research in Texas. *Journal of Suggestive-Accelerative Learning and Teaching*, 1977, *2*.

Caskey, O. L. Suggestology in the United States. *Journal of Suggestive-Accelerative Learning and Teaching*, 1978, *3*.

Gritton, C. E., and R. Benitez-Bordon. Americanizing Suggestopedia: A Preliminary Trial in a U.S. Classroom. *Journal of Suggestive-Accelerative Learning and Teaching*, *1*(2), 83-94.

Kline, P. The Sandy Spring Experiment: Applying Relaxation Techniques to Education. *Journal of Suggestive-Accelerative Learning and Teaching*, Spring 1976, *1*(1), 16-26.

Lozanov, G. A General Theory of Suggestion in the Communications Process and the Activation of the Total Reserves of the Learner's Personality. The First International Congress of Hypnopaedia and Suggesto-hypnopaedia, Paris, France, 1976. English translation by Dr. Gabriel Racle. *Suggestopedia-Canada*, April 1977, 1-4.

Lozanov, G., and P. Balevski. The Effect of the Suggestopedic System of Instruction on the Physical Development, State of Health, and Working Capacity of First and Second Grade Pupils. *Suggestology and Suggestopedia*, 1975, *1*(3), 24-32.

Pollack, C. Educational Experiment: Therapeutic Pedagogy. *Journal of Suggestive-Accelerative Learning and Teaching*, 1976, *1*(2), 95, 97.

Racle, G. A New Development in Education. *Training 1977*, March 1977, 7-9.

Robinnett, E. *The Effects of Suggestopedia in Increased Foreign Language Achievement*. Unpublished doctoral dissertation, Texas Tech University, 1975.

Truce, G. Suggestibility and Learning. *Intellect*, March 1975, *102*, 350-351.

Whole-Brain Learning

Annett, M., and A. Turner. Laterality and the Growth of Intellectual Abilities. *British Journal of Educational Psychology*, Fall 1974, *44*, 37-46.

Ayers, A. J. *The Challenge of the Brain*. ERIC ED104875, August 1971.

Bakan, P. The Right Brain Is the Dreamer. *Psychology Today*, November 1976, *10*(6), 66-68.

Buck, C. Knowing the Left from the Right. *Human Behavior*, June 1976, *5*(6), 29-35.

Foster, S. Hemisphere Dominance and the Art Process. *Art Education*, February 1977, *30*, 28-29.

Grady, M. P. Students Need Media for a Balanced Brain. *Audiovisual Instruction*, November 1976, *21*, 46-48.

Guyer, B. LaRue, and M. P. Friedman. Hemispheric Processing and Cognitive Styles in Learning-Disabled Children. *Child Development*, September 1975, *46*, 658-668.

Iannazzi, M. Brain Asymmetry. *Science Teacher*, January 1975, *42*(1), 47-48.

Mintzberg, H. Planning on the Left Side and Managing on the Right. *Harvard Business Review*, July/August 1967, 49-58.

Nelson, G. K. Concomitant Effects of Visual, Motor, and Verbal Experiences in Young Children's Concept Development. *Journal of Educational Psychology*, August 1976, *68*, 466-473.

Olson, M.B. Right or Left Hemisphere Information Processing in Gifted Students. *The Gifted Child Quarterly*, Spring 1977, *21*, 116-121.

Phillips, M. Confluent Education, the Hidden Curriculum,

and the Gifted Child. *Phi Delta Kappan*, November 1976, *58*, 238-240.

Piaget, J. *The Grasp of Consciousness*. Translated by Susan Wedgwood. Cambridge, Massachusetts: Harvard University Press, 1976.

Regelski, T. A. Who Knows Where Music Lurks in the Mind of Man? New Brain Research Has the Answer. *Music Educators Journal*, May 1977, *63*, 30-38.

Rennels, M. R. Help—My Eyes Are Melting. *Viewpoints*, May 1976, *53*(3), 63-73.

Sage, W. The Split Brain. *Human Behavior*, June 1976, *5*(6), 25-28.

Samples, R. E. Learning with the Whole Brain. *Human Behavior*, February 1975, *4*(2), 16-23.

Schnitker, M. *The Teacher's Guide to the Brain and Learning*. San Rafael, California: Academic Therapy Publications, 1974.

Sperry, R. Messages from the Laboratory. *Academic Therapy*, Winter 1975-76, *11*, 149-155.

Virshup, E. Art and the Right Hemisphere. *Art Education*, November 1976, *29*, 14-15.

Weingartner, C. Ready on the Right. *Media and Methods*, February 1977, *13*, 20-22.

Relaxation

Benson, H. *The Relaxation Response*. New York: Avon, 1976.

Benson, H., J. F. Beary, and M. P. Carol. The Relaxation Response. *Psychiatry*, February 1974, *37*(1), 37-46.

Bernstein, D.A., and T.D. Borkover. *Progressive Relaxation Training: A Manual for the Helping Professions*. Champaign, Illinois: Research Press, 1975.

Frederick, A. B. Biofeedback and Tension Control. *Journal of Physical Education and Recreation*, October 1975, *46*, 25-28.

Frederick, A. B. *Relaxation: A Fourth 'R' for Education.* ERIC ED106261, 1975.

Hoopes, A. T. *Splashdown to Reading.* ERIC ED077171, 1973.

Lupin, M. *et al.* Children, Parents, and Relaxation Tapes. *Academic Therapy,* Fall 1976, *12,* 105-113.

McKim, R. H. Relaxed Attention. *Journal of Creative Behavior,* 1974, *8*(4), 265-276.

O'Rourke, R. Yes, We *Can* Help Kids Relax. *Learning,* 1976, *5*(4), 24-25.

Reinking, R. H., and M. L. Kohl. The Effects of Various Forms of Relaxation Training on Physiological and Self-Report Measures of Relaxation. *Journal of Consulting and Clinical Psychology,* October 1975, *43*(5), 595-600.

Volpe, R. Feedback Facilitated Relaxation Training in School Counseling. *Canadian Counselor,* June 1975, *9*(3), 202-212.

Wallace, J. M. Health Education in the Field of Adult Education. *Adult Education,* May 1974, *47*(1), 10-16.

Fantasy and Imagination

Bodem, M. M. The Role of Fantasy in Children's Reading. *Elementary English,* April 1975, *52*(4), 470-471.

Canfield, J., and P. Klimer. Guided Imagery in the Classroom. *Journal of Humanistic and Transpersonal Education,* 1977, *1*(1).

Castillo, G. A. *Left-Handed Teaching: Lessons in Affective Education.* New York: Praeger, 1974.

Clark, F. V. Fantasy and Imagination. In *Four Psychologies Applied to Education: Freudian, Behavioral, Humanistic, Transpersonal,* edited by Thomas Roberts. New York: John Wiley and Sons, 1975.

Clark, F. V. Learning Through Fantasy. In *Transpersonal Education: A Curriculum for Feeling and Being,* edited by G. Hendricks and J. Fadiman. Englewood Cliffs, New Jersey: Prentice-Hall, Inc., 1976.

Crossley, R. Education and Fantasy. *College English*, 1975, *37*(3), 281-293.

Durio, H. F. Mental Imagery and Creativity. *Journal of Creative Behavior*, 1975, *9*(4), 233-244.

Hendricks, G., and T. B. Roberts. *The Second Centering Book*. Englewood Cliffs, New Jersey: Prentice-Hall, Inc., 1977.

Hendricks, G., and R. Wills. *The Centering Book: Awareness Activities for Children, Parents, and Teachers*. Englewood Cliffs, New Jersey: Prentice-Hall, Inc., 1975.

Hoper, C.-J., U. Kutzleb, A. Stobbe, and B. Weber. *Awareness Games: Personal Growth Through Group Interaction*. New York: St. Martin's Press, 1974.

Khatena, J. Imagination Imagery of Children and the Production of Analogy. *Gifted Child Quarterly*, Winter 1975, *19*, 310-315.

Messon, P. Imagination in Art and Art Education. *Journal of Aesthetic Education*, October 1975, *9*, 55-68.

Pressley, G. M. Mental Imagery Helps Eight-Year-Olds Remember What They Read. *Journal of Educational Psychology*, June 1976, *68*, 355-359.

Curriculum Resources

Abernethy, K., J. Cowley, H. Gilland, and J. Whiteside. *Jumping Up and Down*. San Rafael, California: Academic Therapy Publications, 1970.

Allen, C., and R. Van Allen. *Language Experiences in Early Childhood*. Chicago: Encyclopaedia Britannica Press, 1966.

Allen, J., E. McNeill, and V. Schmidt. *Cultural Awareness for Young Children at the Learning Tree*. Dallas: The Learning Tree, 1975.

Charlip, R., and J. Joyner. *Thirteen.* New York: Parent's Magazine Press, 1975.

Farnette, C., I. Forte, and B. Loss. *Kids' Stuff: Reading and Writing Readiness.* Nashville: Incentive Publications, Inc., 1975.

Flemming, B. M., and D. S. Hamilton. *Resources for Creative Teaching in Early Childhood Education.* New York: Harcourt Brace Jovanovich, Inc., 1977.

Flowers, A. M. *The Big Book of Language Through Sounds.* Danville, Illinois: Interstate Printers and Publishers, Inc., 1972.

Flowers, A. M. *The Big Book of Sounds.* Danville, Illinois: Interstate Printers and Publishers, Inc., 1974.

Grayson, M.F. *Let's Do Fingerplays.* Washington, D.C.: Robert B. Luce, Inc., 1962.

Jacobs, L. *Just Around the Corner.* New York: Holt, Rinehart, and Winston, 1964.

Johnson, E., C. E. Scott, and E. R. Sickles. *Anthology of Children's Literature.* Boston: Houghton Mifflin Co., 1970.

Lewis, S., and J. Reinach. *The Headstart Book of Knowing and Naming.* New York: McGraw-Hill Book Co., 1966.

Lewis, S., and J. Reinach. *The Headstart Book of Looking and Listening.* New York: McGraw-Hill Book Co., 1966.

Lewis, S., and J. Reinach. *The Headstart Book of Thinking and Imagining.* New York: McGraw-Hill Book Co., 1966.

Mendoza, G., and Z. Mostel. *Sesame Street Book of Opposites.* New York: Platt and Munk, Publishers, 1974.

Rather, L., and M. Swift. *Kindergarten Learning Games.* Minneapolis: T. S. Denison and Company, Inc., 1971.

Schaff, J. *The Language Arts Idea Book.* Pacific Palisades, California: Goodyear Publishing Co., Inc., 1976.

Scott, L. B., and J. J. Thompson. *Rhymes for Fingers and*

Flannelbooks. New York: McGraw-Hill Book Co., 1970.

Ward, L. *The Silver Pony*. Boston: Houghton Mifflin Co., 1973.

Records

Abdurahman, B. *Sound, Rhythm, Rhyme, and Mime for Children*. Vocalion.

Adair, T., and F. Adair. *What a Wonderful Thing Is Me*. Disneyland.

Bock, J. *Songs About Animals*. Golden Records.

Dukas, J. *Stories in Sound*. Golden Records.

Jenkins, E. *Country Games and Rhythms for the Little Ones*. Folkways.

Luther, F. *Funny Animal Songs*. Vocations.

Palmer, H. *Pretend*. Educational Activities, Inc.

Raven, N. *Singing in a Circle and Activity Songs*. Pacific Cascade.

Seeger, P. *American Game and Activity Songs for Children*. Folkways.

Seeger, P. *Birds, Beasts, Bugs, and Little Fishes*. Folkways.

White, R. *Play Time Rhythm*. Rhythm Productions.

V.

APPENDIX

MUSIC SELECTIONS FOR CLASS BACKGROUND

In addition to the works of composers referred to earlier, which are recommended generally or for specific use with class activities, a number of other recordings have been found appropriate for various suggestive-accelerative applications. Some of the ones most often utilized as background music are listed below. Some of the performances are lengthy, others relatively short. Some are performed by single artists, others by concert orchestras or symphonies. All fit the major requirements of being relaxed without being "deadly," and pleasant but not demanding of complete attention. Rarely is a work used in its entirety, unless it is a brief one. A practical approach is to repeat, or "loop," a shorter selection several times in order to provide the desired length. Most frequently, several selections are used to make up the 20- to 25-minute span for the visual imagery or relaxation portion of the typical class or session. Hopefully, those selected blend together. Often, music backgrounds are used throughout class periods, and occasionally teachers use the music as a continual background throughout the day. The use of specifically recorded 90-minute (45 minutes on each side) cassettes has been found to be the most practical for the latter applications.

There obviously are almost unlimited possibilities of background music available. It would be possible for someone with the interest and talent to compose special music for specific classroom applications in much the same way as musical scores for plays are written. This would be particularly helpful for use with children. At the moment, however, most teachers applying suggestive-accelerative techniques use what seems appropriate from what is immediately available. Some of these are:

Compositions:
      "Alborado del Garacioso" (Ravel)
      "Clair de Lune" (Debussy)
      "Concerto No. 23 in A Major" (Mozart)
      "Daphnis et Chloe, Suite #2" (Ravel)
      "Fantasia on 'Greensleeves'" (Vaughn-Williams)
      "Fantasia for Harpsichord" (Telemann)
      "Quartet in D" (Hayden)
      "Ich Ruf Zu Dir, Herr Jesu Christ" (Bach)
      "Jesu, Joy of Man's Desiring" (Bach)
      "L'Arlesienne Suites" (Bizet)
      "La Valse" (Ravel)
      "Le Bourgeois Gentilhomme" (Strauss)
      "Lute Suite in E" (Bach)

"Metamorphosen" (Strauss)
"Nocturne from A Midsummer Night's Dream" (Mendelssohn)
"Num Kommí Der Heiden Heiland" (Bach)
"Oboe Concerto" (Hayden)
"Pavan for a Dead Princess" (Ravel)
"Peer Gynt Suite #1, op. 46" (Grieg)
"Peer Gynt Suite #2, op. 55" (Grieg)
"Prelude and Allegro in E Flat" (Bach)
"Quartet in D" (Hayden)
"Serenade in D Minor, op. 44" (Dvorák)
"Sheep May Safely Graze" (Bach)
"Sleepers Awake" (Bach)
"Symphony #44 in E Minor" (Hayden)
"Wind Song—Daphne of the Dunes" (Partch)

Selections from Albums:
"Christopher Parkening Plays Bach" (Christopher Parkening)
"A Day in the Life" (Wes Montgomery)
"Help Me Make It Through the Night" (Hank Crawford)
"The Best of Hank Crawford" (Hank Crawford)
"Bach and Mozart" (Dinu Lipatti)
"Beethoven and Mozart" (Walter Gieseking)
"A Bach Recital" (Andres Segovia)
"Bach—The Goldberg Variation" (Martin Galling)
"Bach Goldberg Variations" (Anthony Newman)
"The Classical Brazilian Guitar" (Maria Liuia)
"The Sounds of India" (Riva Shankar)
"Spectrum Suite" (Steve Halpern)
"I" (Steve Halpern)
"Light and Love and Power" (Joel Andrews)
"Inside" (Paul Horn)

SUGGESTIVE-ACCELERATIVE
CLASS ACTIVITY OUTLINE
(Pre-School Through High School)

In planning suggestive-accelerative learning activities for school presentation, an activity outline is helpful, even for experienced teachers. While it would be desirable for outlines to be placed on activity cards, perhaps the 5 x 8 inch size, for convenience, frequently the outline is too long for filing in this format. Teachers who are more experienced with suggestive-accelerative activities can leave out some sections or abbreviate the outline in order to use the activity card approach. While the format may seem involved for typical classroom use, it is very helpful for teachers who are not familiar with the exercise to be used in the class. The outline which serves quite well in activities of all types and at all levels is summarized below.

Name of Activity or Exercise

Subject:	Identify the activity or exercise to be carried out.
Prerequisites:	List what the student (or class) should know or be able to do in order to carry out the activity or exercise.
Grade Level:	The appropriate age level or grade level for the activity.
Objectives:	List the purposes of the activity and what you are trying to teach with the exercise.
Materials Needed:	List the materials needed in order to carry out the activity or exercise.
Presentation:	List the step-by-step presentation of the activity.
Control of Error:	List how the student knows if the activity is done correctly or not. What type of feedback is planned? Control of error should be in the activity or material used and not with the teacher.
Variations:	How else may the exercise or activity be used: How may the activity be expanded or changed to teach students in different ways or expand knowledge in other areas?
Home Application:	For young children, identify ways in which parents may use the activity to reinforce learning at home. For older students, indicate how they may use the activity in ways which will be interesting or helpful outside of class.

DAILY CLASS RELAXATION SEQUENCE
Progressive Relaxation Type

Sit in your chair with both feet flat on the floor. Place your hands on your lap, and just start relaxing. Begin deep, regular, rhythmic breathing. I will count from one to five. Inhale deeply with the count, hold it, then exhale slowly as I count from one to five. Ready? Inhale— 2–3–4–5. Hold. Now exhale–2–3–4–5. Again, inhale–2–3–4–5. Hold. Exhale–2–3–4–5. Once more. Inhale–2–3–4–5. Hold. Exhale –2–3–4–5.

Fine. Now you are becoming very relaxed. There is a very comfortable feeling coming over you. Let your eyes close very slowly, if you have not done so. Take another deep breath, hold, exhale. Relax. Continue to relax as you concentrate on the sensation of floating, floating, down through your chair. Floating, floating, floating. Downward, downward, downward. A good, heavy, relaxed feeling. Feel how relaxed and loose you are.

I am going to count once more as you relax more and more deeply, more and more completely. Ready—inhale—2–3–4–5. Hold. Exhale—2–3–4–5. Your whole body is more and more relaxed. Breathe deeply again and allow yourself to relax as much as you can. Deeper and deeper. Floating downward. Very calm. Very relaxed. Very serene. Very peaceful.

In this relaxed state, you experience a feeling of well-being and optimism that allows you to absorb new ideas more easily, to retain them longer, and repeat them readily. Maintain your body relaxation while your mind becomes more calm, more tranquil, eliminating all discordant thoughts. Breathe deeply. Calm and peaceful. Relaxing physically and mentally. Inhale—2–3–4–5. Now exhale. More and more relaxed, more and more receptive to the new material and ideas which will be presented to you. I am going to count backward from five to one as you become more and more relaxed.

Ready. 5—more and more relaxed, 4—relaxing physically and mentally, 3—floating down, very calm and peaceful, 2—a very pleasant feeling of floating and relaxing, and 1—now you are relaxed, yet alert—a condition which allows you to be at your creative best. Very relaxed.

Very relaxed, very receptive. Savor this pleasant feeling as you repeat these ideas to yourself:

   —Say to yourself, "I, and only I, have control over my senses and faculties."
   —Say, "If I am called, I can respond immediately and effectively."
   —Repeat this idea, "I can become absorbed in new ideas and material."
   —Say, "I can eliminate all distracting and disturbing thoughts."
   —Say, "My mind is clear and calm."
   —Repeat this idea, "I can think clearly and concentrate easily."
   —Say, "I can improve my abilities and memory."
   —Say to yourself, "I have confidence in myself."
   —Repeat that idea again, "I have confidence in myself."

Now you are relaxed, but alert. Calm, but attentive. If you have difficulty recalling any material covered today, simply take a deep breath, exhale slowly, and say to yourself—"relax." You will find that what you are trying to remember will return much more readily. Now I am going to count from one to three. At the count of three, let your eyes open but retain your relaxed and tranquil feeling, while maintaining your state of alertness and awareness, as your teacher presents new and interesting material to you.

Ready—1—2—3. Let your eyes open. Everyone now listen with attention and interest to the new material. (Elapsed time—approximately 6-1/2 minutes. Continue with presentation of new material.)

- - - - - - - - - - - - - - - (Presentation of New Material) - - - - - - - - - - - - - - -

(End of class.) All right. Now everyone let your eyes close once more. Take a deep breath, exhale slowly. Relax and allow what you have learned to sink inward, slowly, deeply, indelibly.

Now I am going to count from one to five. At the count of five, let your eyes open and return to your normal state of awareness; refreshed, alert, feeling good. You will feel wide awake, energetic. You will feel stronger and more capable. You will find it easier to be cheerful and optimistic. Your work will go better and easier. You will feel better than you have felt before. Ready—1—more and more alert, 2—feeling stronger and better, 3—returning to your normal state of awareness, 4—happy and confident, and 5—open your eyes everyone. You feel very good. Very refreshed. This feeling will persist for some time to come. This is the end of the session.

SENSE FOCUSING
(Elementary and Above)

Sit as comfortably as you can and relax. Breathe naturally and easily. Close your eyes and imagine the things I describe as clearly as you can. Imagine that you are in a dimly lit room which has only a chair and a table. See yourself sitting in the chair at the table. On the table is a lemon.

See the lemon on the brown, bare wood of the table. It is bright yellow and shiny. Pick up the lemon and hold it in your hand, turning it over and over. Look at it very carefully. Notice the texture of the skin. See all the small dots on the surface, the bump at one end, and the place where it was attached to the tree making a small indentation at the other end. Look at it carefully.

Bring the lemon near your nose and smell it. Now put it down on the table. You have a knife. Very slowly, cut the lemon in half. Notice the backward and forward movement of the knife as it cuts into the lemon. See the small drops of juice coming from the cut and clinging to the knife blade.

Pick up a part of the lemon. Look at it carefully. Notice where the lemon is cut. Look at the white part, the sections, the texture. Take the piece of lemon and bring it to your mouth. Squeeze it and taste the tangy flavor. Hold the lemon juice in your mouth as you taste the strong, citric flavor and smell the piece of lemon held in your hand. Now, open your eyes and return to the here and now. Return to the people around you.

****

Discuss the taste sensations resulting from the exercise the first time it is used in class.

Have students share their feelings. Was anyone not able to see and taste the lemon? If students are old enough, discuss the relation between tangible and fantasy experiences. Which are "real"? How do you know? Share feelings and experiences, if possible. This exercise can be used a number of times during a semester or course to help students see how their abilities in mental imagery and sense impressions are improving.

ENVIRONMENTAL WALK–
VISUAL IMAGERY EXERCISE
The Mountain Valley

This is an exercise in using your imagination while relaxing. Sit in your chair as comfortably as you can, breathe easily and normally, and begin to relax. Move your feet around until you find a comfortable position. Hold your arms at your sides, shake them vigorously, and then fold them comfortably in your lap. Let your head fall to your chest, close your eyes, breathe deeply, and relax.

I am going to describe a quiet mountain valley, and I want you to visualize it as clearly as you can. I will describe many of the details, but you will need to fill in a number of them yourself. Use your imagination to sense as many of the experiences which are described as possible.

Imagine that you are standing, looking over a quiet, beautiful, green, mountain valley. As you look across the valley, you see the mountains rising in the distance. They stretch to a deep, blue sky in which soft, white, fluffy clouds float. You see snow on the tops of some of the mountains and where it remains in the crevasses of the rocks. Down the mountainside, there are trees in greens and golds and browns. You notice green pines rising to the sky. Beautifully shaped fir and spruce trees in other shades of green dot the mountainside. Aspens grow in clumps among the pines with colors of gold and yellow sparkling in the sun. Down the side of the mountain among the trees, a stream flows vigorously, emptying into the green meadow. You see the white froth of the water bubbling over multi-colored rocks, providing shining shades of black, brown, red, and gray.

There is a lush carpet of green grass in the meadow. It is the late fall, yet many flowers still bloom. You notice colors of white and pink and purple as the flowers bloom along the stream and in clumps among the green grass.

Imagine yourself sitting by the stream. You are sitting, leaning against a sturdy pine tree which grows near the water's edge. The sun filters through the pine, and you feel its warmth on your face and shoulders. You enjoy the smells of pines and flowers brought to you on a cool breeze. You feel the breeze gently across your face as you watch the grass wave in the meadow. As you watch, a leaf carried by the wind floats gently toward the stream. It falls gently on the water, where it is caught in the current. You watch the leaf bounce along the rocks floating down the stream. You watch as the leaf floats out of sight.

You lean back against the tree, feeling the rough bark between your shoulders and the soft grass providing a cushion. You close your eyes, listening to the sounds of birds and the wind murmuring in the pine needles. The cool breeze and the warm sun caress your face, while you enjoy the sounds and the smells which surround you in the valley. You sit there quietly relaxing, at ease, comfortable, at peace with yourself.

Now, gently open your eyes and return to those around you, maintaining this quiet, peaceful, comfortable feeling which you have experienced in the mountain valley.

VISUAL IMAGERY—BUILD-ON RESPONSES

Children sit or lie in a circle with eyes closed and relaxing to music background.

Teacher starts by making an "it makes me think of" statement. Other children (in turns or spontaneously) add additional "it makes me think of" statements linked to the previous one. Children should know that it is all right to "pass," if responses are in sequence.

Example: Teacher: "Snow makes me think of winter."

Child A: "Winter makes me think of Christmas."
Child B: "Christmas makes me think of toys."
Child C: "Toys make me think of a bicycle."
　etc.

Continue until all children have had an opportunity to make an additional "it makes me think of" statement or the topic has gone around the circle. Discuss images that accompanied the responses ("Did you 'see' each of the thoughts suggested by others? Which ones were easy to visualize? Which ones were hard to visualize?"). Share images, if appropriate.

Variation: Have children share the reason they think of each ending by adding a "because" element to each statement ("Winter makes me think of ice because I like to ice skate.").

Sample "it makes me think of" stems:
Books make me think of ... (because ...).
Airplanes make me think of ... (because ...).
Ice cream makes me think of ... (because ...).
Boats make me think of ... (because ...).
Elephants make me think of ... (because ...).
Boots make me think of ... (because ...).
Rain makes me think of ... (because ...).

VISUAL IMAGERY MEMORY EXERCISE
(All Levels)

Class relaxes to music background with eyes closed.

Class is told they are going to listen to a short story about a picture. Everyone is to imagine the picture and all the things about the story, remembering as much as they can.

The teacher (and later perhaps students can take turns) selects a picture which, although not too complex, does contain several objects and/or persons. The students should not have seen the picture before. Pictures may come from magazines, calendars, or specially made by the teacher from a collection of smaller pictures of objects. A picture book, such as *The Silver Pony* by Lynd Ward, makes an excellent collection of picture stimulus material for young children.

The picture provides the stimulus for a brief, simple story using all the objects and people in the picture. The students listen as the story is told, but do not see the picture. The story may be repeated, if necessary.

The story is discussed, with the teacher using questions, if required, to bring out all the objects and people involved in the story and that appear in the picture. The class should agree on all the elements appearing in the story.

When the elements have been discussed, students again visualize the picture and then each draw a picture (or groups of four or five students may cooperate in drawing a picture) to illustrate the story. The teacher then has students compare the pictures they have made with the one originally used as the picture stimulus, which they now see for the first time.

Variation: A group of students may be asked if they would like to act out the story, if it is an appropriate one to use in this manner.

Note: This exercise may be quite simple or very complex depending on the picture selected and the story developed to go with it. The younger the child, the simpler the picture and story, is a good general principle to follow. Always emphasize the drawing as a good representation of what the student heard and visualized, and that each one is important. Avoid comparisons and evaluative comments on their efforts.

VISUAL IMAGERY—THE LIVING PAINTING

Choose a painting, picture, or photograph (preferably a large one with clear details). Use a music background in keeping with the theme of the picture. Children sit in a circle where each can see the picture clearly.

After everyone has studied the picture, ask the group to identify all the objects that are in the picture. Have children name and identify as carefully as can be done, with children adding descriptions ("There is a bird." "A blue bird." "A big, blue bird." "A big, blue bird flying over the house.") for details or action. Allow any assumptions that are accurate or reasonable ("Flying very fast.").

When all of the major elements have been identified, ask children to close their eyes and see if they can visualize the picture as clearly as they can. Look at the picture and close eyes alternately, until there is a clear image of the picture when eyes are closed.

Children continue to imagine the picture and focus on other sense impressions ("Are there things in the picture which remind you of sounds? of smells? of tastes?").

"Now imagine that *you* are *in* the picture. Answer these questions to yourself:
    —Where would you be?
    —What would you be doing?

–What would you be hearing?

–What would you be smelling?

–What would you be tasting?" (Add other questions related to the picture.)

Option Ending A: "Open your eyes and continue to think about the picture. Make a drawing of anything the picture reminds you of, but do not just copy the picture. You may want to draw something from the picture or something you imagined. You may want to draw something that happened before the picture or will happen after the picture."

Option Ending B: Same as above, but write a story about the picture. Include what led up to the picture, what is happening in the picture, and what will happen after the picture. Write about what you imagine the ending of the story will be.

Option Ending C: Have students share their images and impressions with the class or in small groups of four to eight students.

Option Ending D: Use visual imagery and pictures to lead into a topic for discussion on the subject of the lesson. Make posters, develop books, or engage in other activities related to the subject area involved.

VISUAL IMAGERY
AND CREATIVE WRITING EXERCISES
(Grade 3 and Above)

Variation 1. Class relaxes to music background with eyes closed. The teacher reads a story which the class has not heard before. It should be one which can provide several logical endings, or the story should be read only to a point where a number of events could logically transpire. Children listen to the story and visualize the events and persons as vividly as possible. The story may be repeated, if necessary.

Ask class to visualize what happens next–or how the story ends. Ask them to think of several ways the story might go. Think about them and then select one to write about. Think the next step in the story or the ending of the story through in detail, using your imagination. Go over it several times in your mind.

The students open their eyes and write the story. When all have written the story ending, share endings and discuss. Talk about how visual imagery helped in deciding how the story would end and how to write about it. Children can also be asked to draw a picture to illustrate their story "ending."

Variation 2. Class relaxes to music background with eyes closed. Teacher provides a detailed description of a picture which the class has not seen. Children imagine the picture as vividly as possible in all its details. They think about a story which would go with the picture, one for which the picture could be used as an illustration. They visualize the story in as much detail as possible.

The students open their eyes. They write the story they have selected to go with the picture. They may also be asked to draw a picture which they think will be like the one the teacher described.

The class discusses how imagery helped form the story outline. They share the stories which have been written (and drawings, if used). The teacher then shares the original picture with the class.

Variation 3. Class relaxes to music background with eyes closed. Students are asked to visualize a story they will write on an assigned topic. The writing assignment is made and students imagine the story they will write in as much detail as possible. They are to think of all the elements and make mental images of how they would appear in the story. Writing assignments, such as tall tales, vacation experiences, animal stories, science fiction, "why" or "if" stories, or other topics appropriate to the level of the students, may be used.

Students are to think through the story sequence they intend to write about from beginning to end. Have them go over it several times to be sure they see how it will all fit together.

The students open their eyes and write the stories.

They discuss visual images and how the story emerged while thinking about it. Share the stories which have been written. Draw pictures to go with their stories.

Variation 4. Class relaxes to music background with eyes closed. The students are told that the music will be changed, and they are to continue to relax and concentrate on the music selection which will be played. The teacher selects music, preferably *not* one used for background music with the class on other occasions, and has students listen to it. Students are asked to visualize a story that might go along with the music. "Think of what kind of story the music reminds you of and visualize it in as much detail as possible. Go over it several times in your mind. Develop a story which fits the music, like a movie or television story fits the music played in the background."

The students open their eyes and write the story selected.

They discuss visual images and how they related to the music and the story. They share the stories which have been written. Have students draw a picture to go with the story.

Option A. Use same procedure as above, but have students write a poem instead of a story to the music.

Option B. Use same procedure as above, but have all students visualize a story or poem and write on the same topic—food, weather, vacation time, pets, animals, etc. Care must be taken to make sure the music used is appropriate for the topic selected.

In the class discussion, find out if any problems resulted from the teacher's selection of a topic which "fit" the music. What type of music would have better suited the topic for the students who had difficulty? Did the music make it easier to think of a story? Visualize it?

OWEN L. CASKEY is Director of the Office of Instructional Research at Texas Tech University, Lubbock, Texas, where he also serves as Associate Dean and Professor of Educational Psychology in the College of Education. His teaching and research activities include areas related to early concept development, academic achievement, values structure, and learning. His baccalaureate and master's degrees were completed at Texas Tech University, and he earned his doctorate at the University of Colorado in 1952, where he also was a post-doctoral fellow in counseling psychology in 1954. He taught at the public school level and in universities in Texas, Oklahoma, and Colorado, as well as serving in departmental and university level administrative positions. He also held positions as director of counseling centers, psychologist for Veteran's Administration Hospitals, psychologist in business and industry, as well as professorships in educational psychology and counseling prior to returning to Texas Tech University in 1964. At Texas Tech, he served as Vice President for Student Affairs and was Associate Vice President for Academic Affairs before returning to research and teaching in his current position in 1973. He has held offices in state, regional, and national counseling and psychological professional associations, currently being President of the Society for Suggestive-Accelerative Learning and Teaching. He has published extensively in books, professional journals, and research publications.